D1244323

AVON FREE PUBLIC LIBRARY
281 COUNTRY CLUB ROAD, AVON CT 06001

MŒBIUS 06

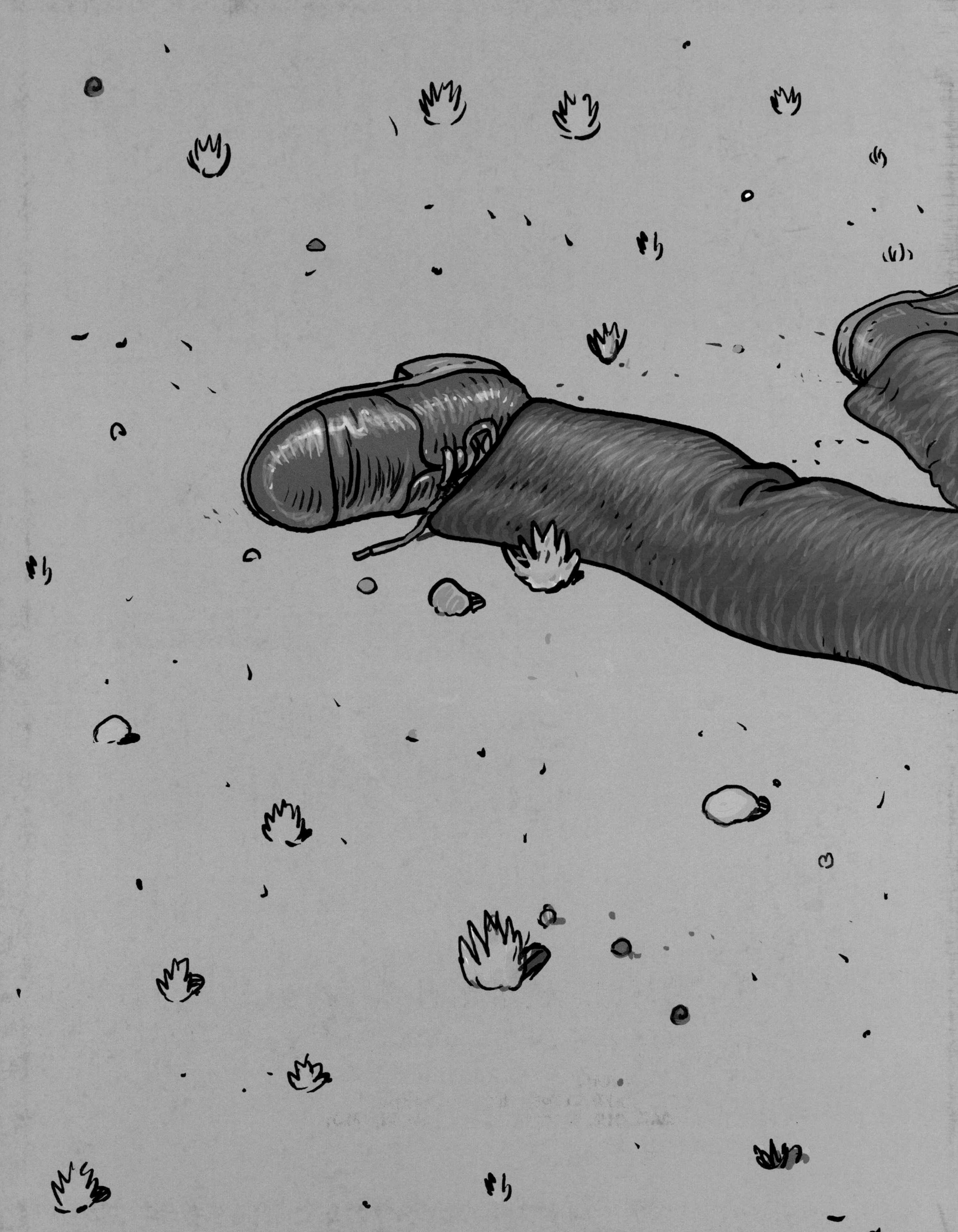

INSIDE ☆ MŒBIUS

PART I

Written and illustrated by
JEAN "MOEBIUS" GIRAUD

Commentary by
ISABELLE GIRAUD and MOEBIUS PRODUCTION

Translation by
DIANA SCHUTZ

Lettering by
ADAM PRUETT

GRAPHIC MOE c-1

AVON FREE PUBLIC LIBRARY
281 COUNTRY CLUB ROAD, AVON CT 06001

MOEB.

DARK HORSE BOOKS

Publisher
MIKE RICHARDSON

Tout Inside Moebius Editor
ISABELLE GIRAUD

Dark Horse Edition Editor
PHILIP R. SIMON

Dark Horse Edition Assistant Editor
MEGAN WALKER

Tout Inside Moebius Designers
CLAIRE CHAMPEVAL and **NAUSICAÄ GIRAUD**

Dark Horse Edition Designer
JUSTIN COUCH with **RICK DeLUCCO**

Digital Art Technician
ADAM PRUETT

Dark Horse's Inside Moebius editions are based on the final French-language collection of this work, *Tout Inside Moebius*, published by Moebius Production.

MOEBIUS LIBRARY: INSIDE MOEBIUS PART 1
Inside Moebius Part 1 © 2018 Moebius Production / Isabelle Giraud. All rights reserved. Dark Horse Books® and the Dark Horse logo are registered trademarks of Dark Horse Comics, Inc. All rights reserved. No portion of this publication may be reproduced or transmitted, in any form or by any means, without the express written permission of Dark Horse Comics, Inc. Names, characters, places, and incidents featured in this publication either are the product of the author's imagination or are used fictitiously. Any resemblance to actual persons (living or dead), events, institutions, or locales, without satiric intent, is coincidental.

Published by
Dark Horse Books
A division of Dark Horse Comics, Inc.
10956 SE Main Street
Milwaukie, OR 97222

DarkHorse.com | Moebius.fr

To find a comics shop in your area,
visit the Comic Shop Locator Service at comicshoplocator.com

First edition: February 2018
ISBN: 978-1-50670-320-6

10 9 8 7 6 5 4 3 2 1

Printed in China

LET ME THROUGH!

FOREWORD

by Isabelle Giraud

From the Earth to the Sky, From the Sky to the Earth

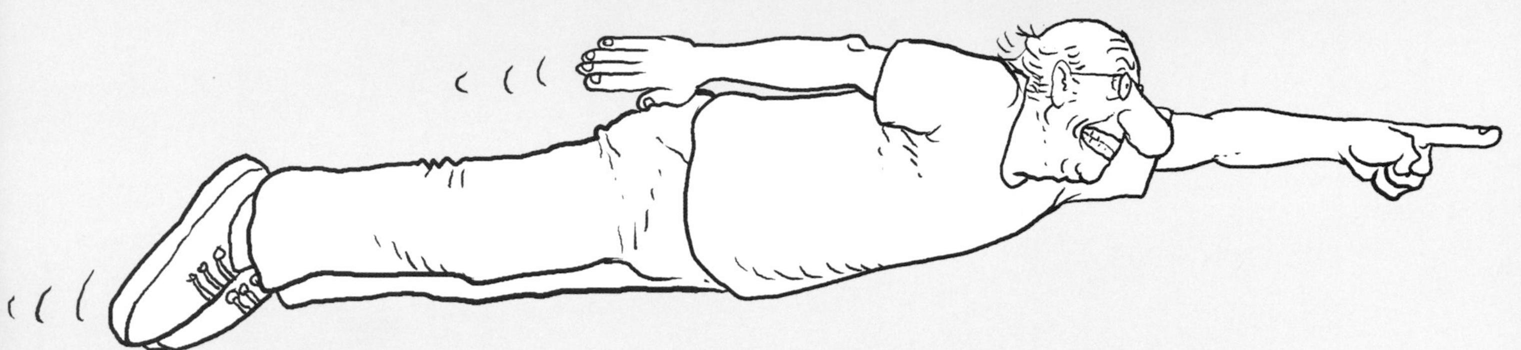

The six volumes of *Inside Moebius* were born between the years 2000 and 2009, unexpectedly emerging from the universe designed for *40 jours dans le désert B* (*40 Days in Desert B*), a book published in 2000 by Stardom.

Through the magic of art, Moebius's resolve to stop smoking weed—and thus to "weed himself out"—provided the landscape for this Desert B, at the heart of which he established a setting for psychic expression.

In *Inside Moebius*, the vast empty space of the blank page is under the total control of the author, who alone has the power to pervade it and the daring, even, to introduce himself within. Down below, at the level of the page, life takes shape exclusively under his will. Up above, at the level of the reader, Moebius well knows he must trust in this angel on high whose perceptivity will be sorely tested.

Fellow readers! Moebius has put you in a choice position. Don't hesitate to read and re-read every single panel, to flip back a few pages, to peruse the previous volume in order to better find and understand the keys to interpreting the story.

Don't be afraid of losing yourself in the Moebius labyrinth: it's the price you pay for the gentle thrill growing between you and the master of the realm, Jean Giraud himself! *He* certainly doesn't hesitate to go the extra mile in this work—the extra *ten* miles—just to please you. He's put all his heart into: unveiling his secrets for you; introducing you to his creative dramas and joys; and ushering you through the door of his "Big Bulletproof Airtight Ego-Bunker"!

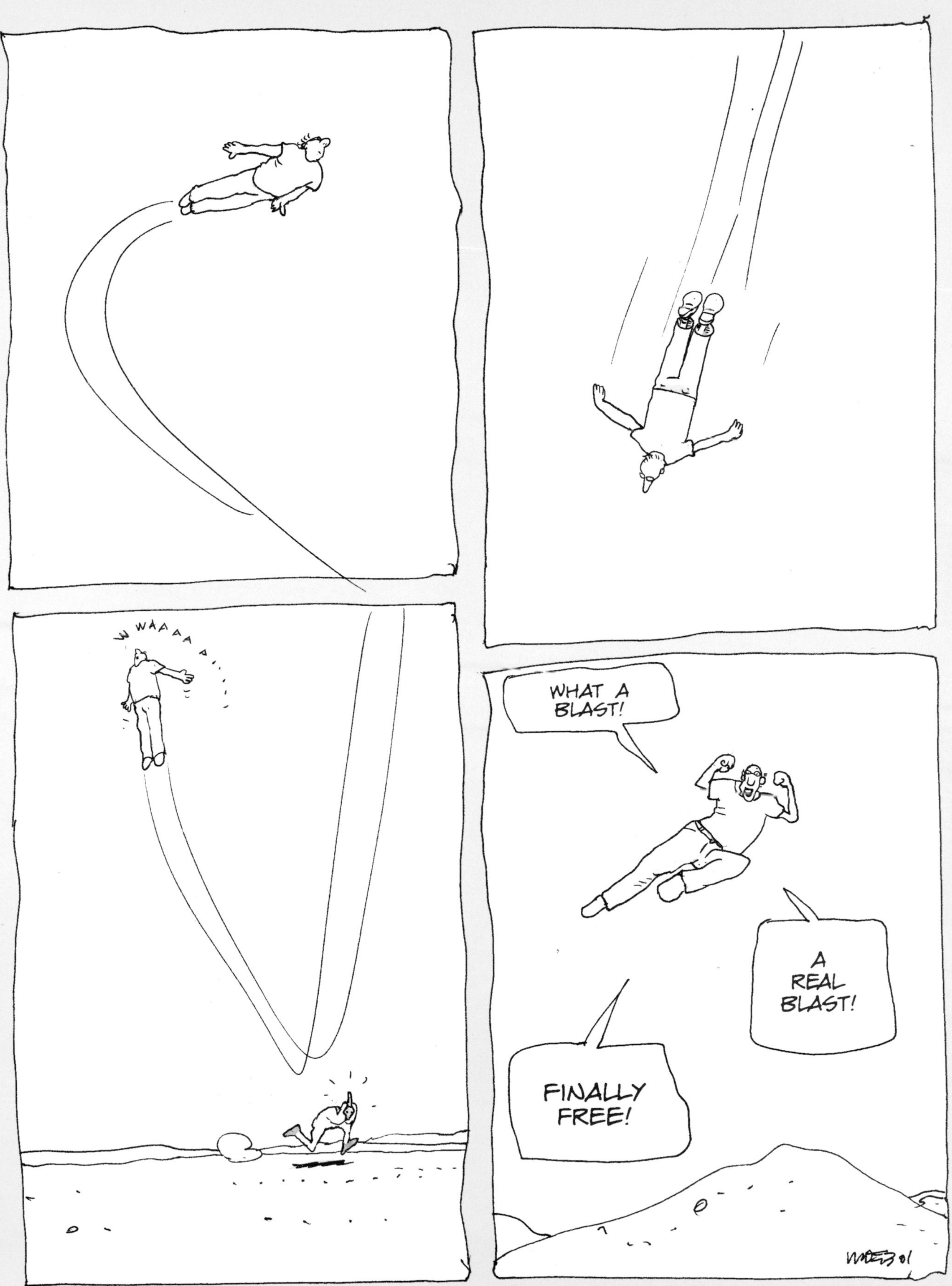
WWAAAAA...
WHAT A BLAST!
A REAL BLAST!
FINALLY FREE!
MOEB '01

Possible Vanishing Point

For its artist, *Inside Moebius* is "a discipline and a technique; it's the result of an entire study extending over years." Its primary graphic methodology is improvisation, of both line and story structure. A rigidity of form isn't necessary. The form emerges bit by bit, gaining its rhythm from the artist's own daily life. It's also a study of point of view and of the effects of perspective generally: "Simply displacing the object of perception is enough to immerse oneself in another state of consciousness." In the vast emptiness of Desert B, everything is possible. It's the ideal space for recording the never-ending to-and-fro between the exterior and interior of the self. For such a multifaceted artist, however, the question of self offers infinite answers. But never mind! It's sufficient to focus on the essential and to surround oneself with beloved characters such as Blueberry, Arzak, the Major, Malvina, Stel, and Atan.

Originally created as a journal in which the author might accurately transcribe his overall impressions of his decision to stop smoking, *Inside Moebius* quickly became "His Autobiographical Œuvre." Jean chooses to use himself as a character—the leading actor—in this adventure. He presents himself as the subject of a story in which he summons his acclaimed creations to the heart of Desert B. As a result, two parallel forces underlie the action, as the author/creator finds himself caught up not only in his "living" reality, but also with his paper creations (and, above all, with Jean Giraud himself).

ACTUALLY, MY NAME IS "UNCONSCIOUS."
I am everywhere and nowhere!
"JEAN-MICHEL" IS JUST MY FIRST NAME!
SO, MY FULL NAME IS "JEAN-MICHEL UNCONSCIOUS."

Getting High

In Desert B, it's very easy for the author to rid himself of spatiotemporal constraints: he can simply fly off, move through designated doors, or fall asleep and wake up in the thick of a dream to begin to find meaning in what's going on. When reality becomes too difficult to bear, it "drops into art," the transcription drawing a path to elucidation. In the second volume of *Inside Moebius Part 1*, Osama bin Laden becomes a character on the page, and he reproaches the Major—himself the quintessential product of Western society—for claiming to represent *all* of humanity and for attempting to impact history by way of this myth—to which the Major responds that the collapse of the Twin Towers will fade from collective memory and the fate of the planet transcends Earth's destiny. The Major's knowledge of an upcoming cosmocivilization helps to put things in perspective for us: fragile humans still bound to earthly events.

Almost every one of the six volumes of *Inside Moebius* either begins or ends with flight. For the author, flying symbolizes the ever-present desire to escape by way of drawing and its deliberations; to throw off gravity's shackles; to rise; to sail over the cares of earthly life. Flying allows him to access other perceptions of reality, to get high indeed, and to search for an answer in dreams. But as with Icarus, sometimes the unexpected precipitates his fall. His dream of flying runs up against physical constraints, and reality supersedes. In this case, in addition to the events of 9/11, Jean also suffered a major physical trauma in 2001, giving him a glimpse of his own mortality. And so, beneath its humorous surface, the second volume of *Inside Moebius* also reveals a dramatic dimension. At the story's end, while the author would prefer to keep flying, Malvina catches up with him and begs him to return home to his bunker.

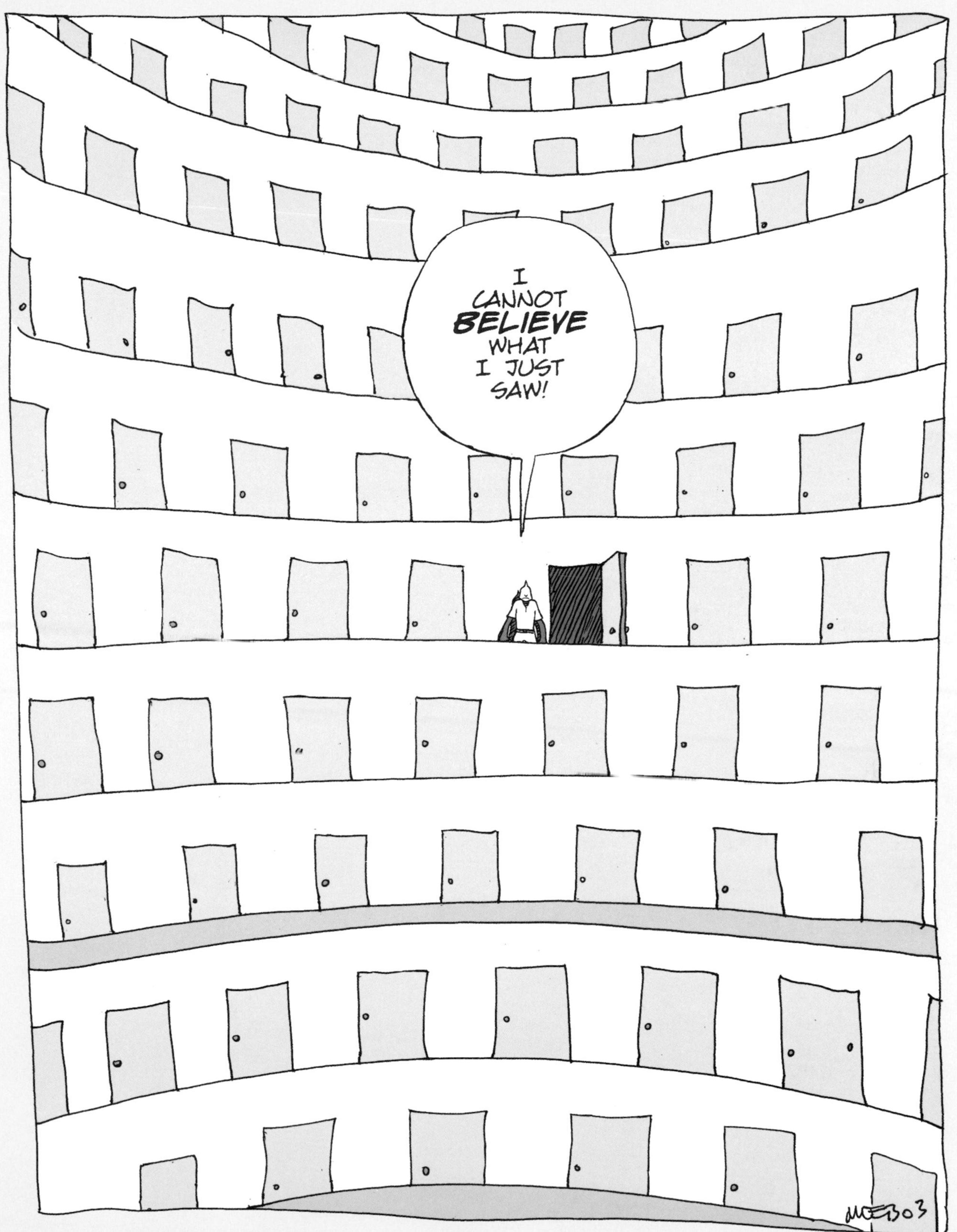
I CANNOT BELIEVE WHAT I JUST SAW!
MŒB03

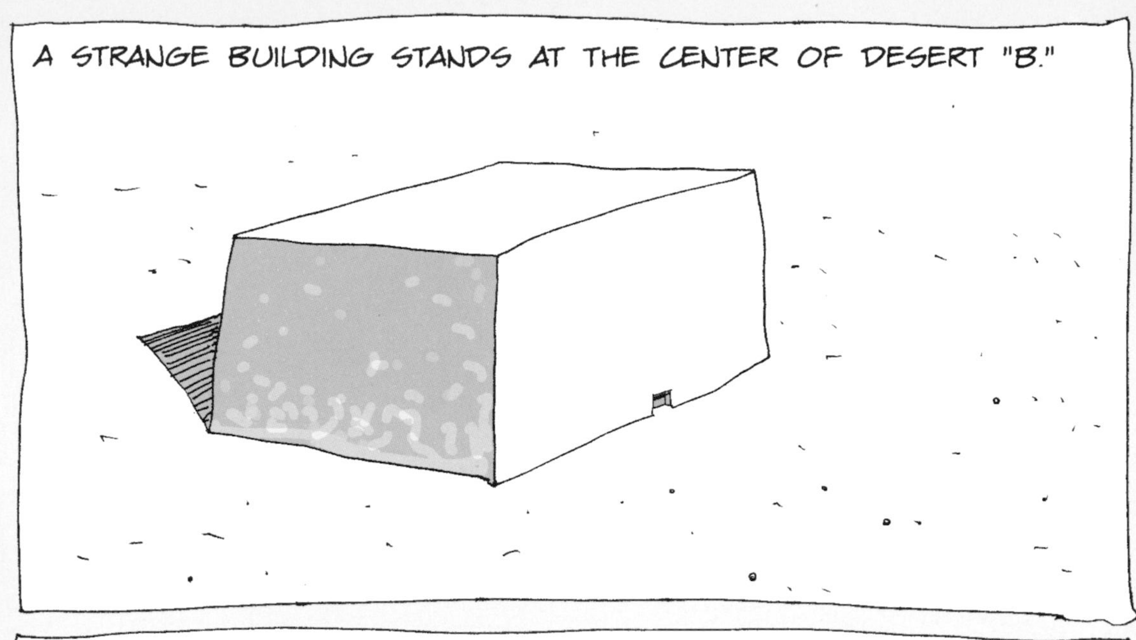
A STRANGE BUILDING STANDS AT THE CENTER OF DESERT "B."

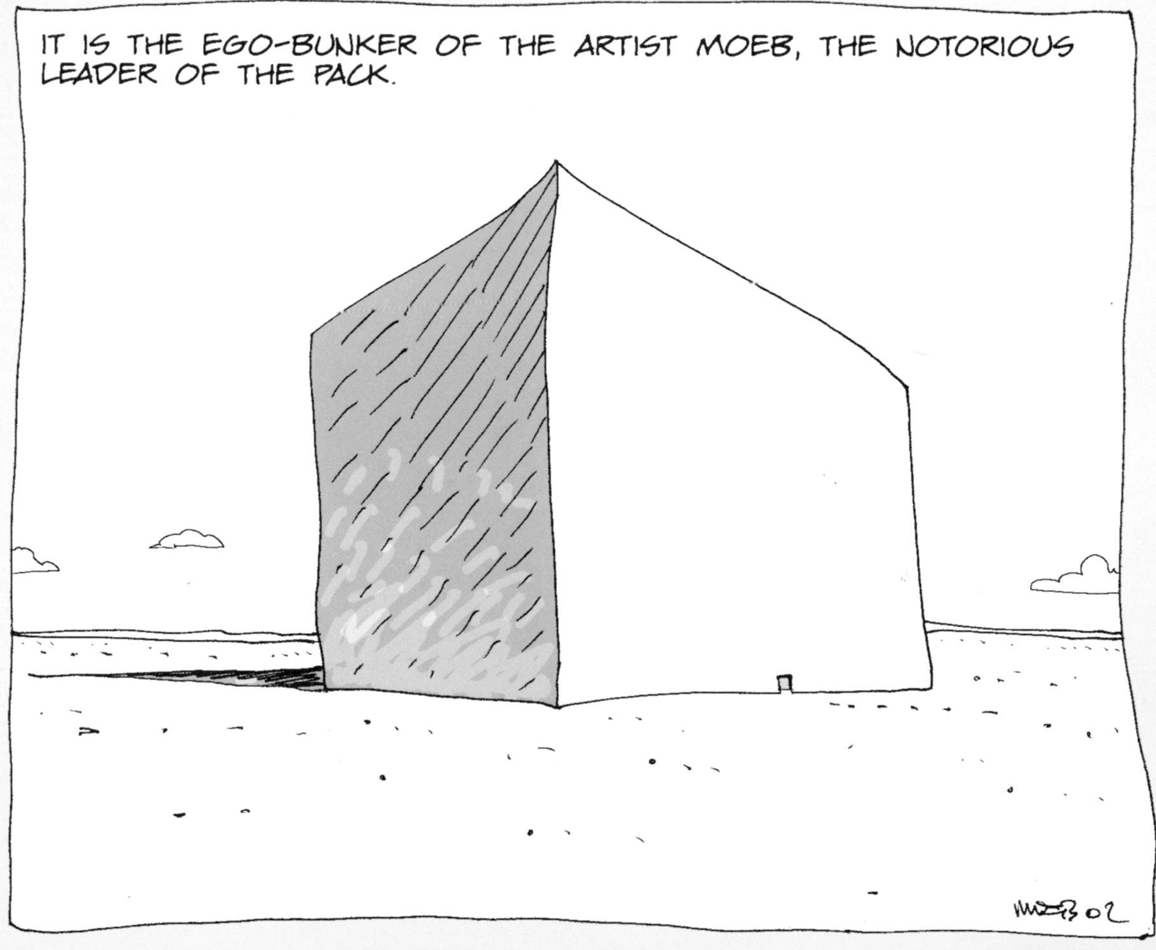
IT IS THE EGO-BUNKER OF THE ARTIST MOEB, THE NOTORIOUS LEADER OF THE PACK.

Ego-Bunker

"It all started back in that icy room of my grandparents . . ."

The Desert B bunker, that monolithic monument appearing in each of the six volumes of *Inside Moebius*, constitutes the absolute refuge: everything is decided here, in this shelter to which Moebius withdraws to make contact with another dimension. His characters also gain entry at times, either at his invitation or because they're desperate for a script. Vexed at being abandoned during the author's retreats, his characters vainly attempt pursuit to prevent him from thinking only of himself. And so they decide to track down and invade the bunker.

This sacred place, subject to all manner of transmutation, allows Moebius to change footing, to wander its infinite corridors, to go through designated doorways, to find a way out. Its interior sometimes resembles a labyrinth, other times a series of nested drawers, corridors, and doors granting passage from one dimension to another, albeit at the risk of losing oneself. The Ego-Bunker may well correspond to the ancient *tumuli*, domelike mounds constructed by Celtic tribes and flanked by a small door allowing human access to a second dimension—from our world to that of the Spirits, those beings who took on the appearance of the "Little People."

We can no doubt see a race of demigods in the figures of Arzak, Blueberry, the Major, Stel, and Atan, thanks to whom the author attains a certain spirituality of his own.

Surviving Oneself

The spatial dimension of *Inside Moebius* is augmented by the temporal. The urgent appeals of his fictional characters provide a soundtrack to the artist's life. Their number, their demands, and their jealousy of each other leads the author to abandon them, conferring instead with his own doubles—especially his 1970s counterpart—who have materialized out of the past. Finding himself face to face with an infinity of selves, the author is prevented from taking his own path . . . to the point of becoming a stranger among all these selves: the "successive" selves, "perpendicular" selves, "folded, multiplied, or divided" selves, the "parallel" selves, the "diagonal" selves . . .

What A Blast!

Moebius takes on existential questions about God, death, illness, and love—including self-love—and tries to find answers in dreaming. He insists, here, on the need to make time for oneself, to let oneself be absorbed—devoured even—by the unconscious in order to truly find oneself. Dreams and the unconscious are themes that recur throughout the author's entire body of work. His ultimate reference text remains *The Art of Dreaming* by Carlos Castaneda. For Moebius, there is no turning back from the effectiveness of his spiritual mentor's method of freeing oneself from all obsessions: and that is, simply, to sleep beside oneself . . .

A LITTLE TALK WITH ISABELLE IN 2004 . . .

Isabelle: Jean, how did the *Inside Moebius* project come to be?

Jean: When I stopped smoking weed, I decided—in part to help strengthen my determination—to record my various impressions, sensations, and reflections arising from this decision. Little by little, as I got into it, that starting point gave way to a new idea: to confront each of my characters by giving them a certain autonomy, and to involve myself with them in a semi-serious game of smoke and mirrors.

I wasn't planning to publish these pages at first, but I wound up having so much fun that I became interested in putting them into print.

Isabelle: It really turned into a *story*?

Jean: I'd say it's more of a journal without any real story (much to the chagrin of the characters). It's a kind of improvisation from day to day and page to page, fed by each day's moods and events.

Isabelle: It's a real comic book nonetheless . . .

Jean: I do use the language and traditional storytelling of comics. The only difference is that I'm working without a net, without a script, that is, or any preliminary penciling, and then sketching it out as quickly as possible to preserve the utmost spontaneity.

Isabelle: Strictly speaking, these are not *sketches* . . .

Jean: No, indeed! There's a pursuit of accuracy in the drawing as well as an ongoing attempt to stay within a certain style, in order to avoid the overly loose, throwaway aspect of sketching. But without preliminary pencils or any redrawing, the art seems fresher to me and more inventive.

Isabelle: Might we think of *Inside Moebius* as a kind of diary?

Jean: In light of literary tradition, of course, there is a certain continuum [to which it belongs], but the comics medium has pretty much already adopted that genre—enough, I'd say, to give it its own distinctiveness. Whereas in the pages of *Inside Moebius*, I turn myself into a character like any other, thereby dissociating him, to some extent, from my real self.

To give life to the character, I supplement him with autobiographical elements and current events, but also with the dreams, sensations, and emotions that I feel when I'm actually drawing. It's a reflection—in a way that I hope is humorous—of the relationship between the author, his inner world, and his characters.

Isabelle: You're not afraid of being accused of narcissism?

Jean: No, because drawing oneself is the equivalent of the writer's first-person "I." There's no reason to exclude comics from that game.

Isabelle: Do you intend to continue this experiment?

Jean: Everything depends on the public's reaction to this first part, of course, but I've already gone through six notebooks and just begun a seventh.

FUMETTI (1)

MOEBIUS
2000

INSIDE MOEBIUS

VOLUME 1

Don't tell me any tall tales! *You* are the author.

In the past it was me . . . Now, in the present,
it's no longer me, but *me in the future* . . .
which is to say, not yet me . . .

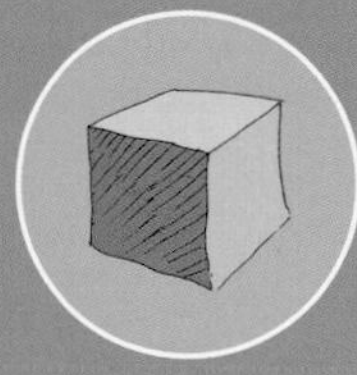

FIRST LESSON:
SMOKING DOES NOT
IMPROVE THE ART.

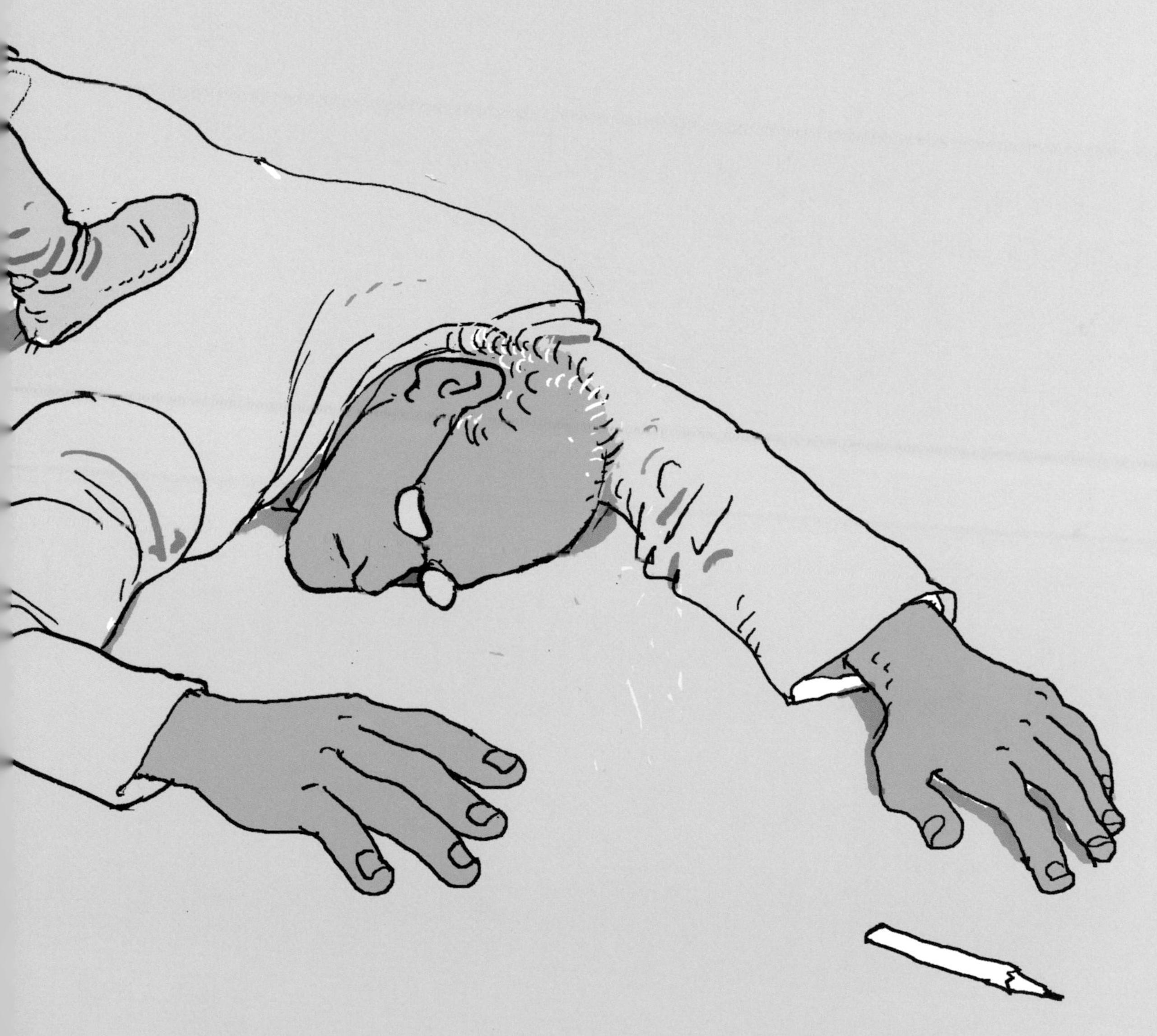

2

WHEN I HAVEN'T SMOKED, I'VE LIVED A NORMAL LIFE.

MY THOUGHTS ABOUT MYSELF ARE NORMAL.
I DO NOT LOVE YOU.
YOU SAID IT!

ON THE OTHER HAND, WHEN I HAVE SMOKED, NOTHING AT ALL IS NORMAL...

...I SEE MYSELF THROUGH THE EYES OF ANOTHER.
I LOVE YOU!
YOU SAID IT!

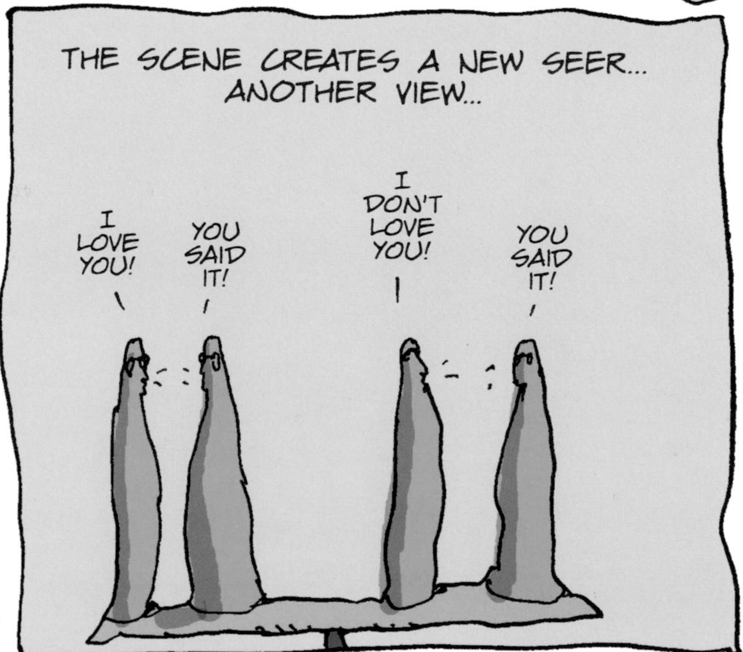
THE SCENE CREATES A NEW SEER... ANOTHER VIEW...
I LOVE YOU!
YOU SAID IT!
I DON'T LOVE YOU!
YOU SAID IT!

IF WE CONTINUE THIS PROCESS OF UNPACKING THE VIEW...

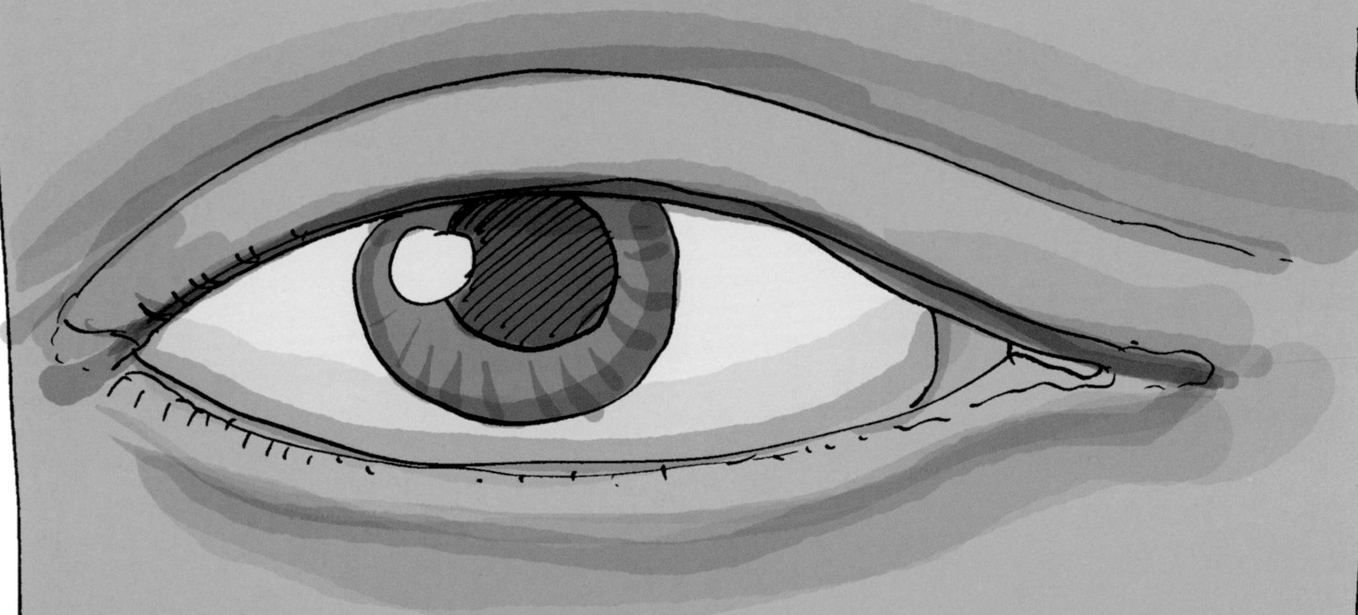

...WE REACH A SORT OF ***ULTIMATE*** VIEW
GENERALLY SYMBOLIZED BY HALF A PAIR OF EYES. BUT,
AFTER ALL, THIS IS JUST A CONVENTION OF LANGUAGE.

FOR ME, SMOKING TAKES ON A SACRED ASPECT...

...BUT I MUST SMOKE TO REMEMBER THAT.

5
STOPPING SMOKING IS EASY!
ESPECIALLY AFTER HAVING SMOKED.

6

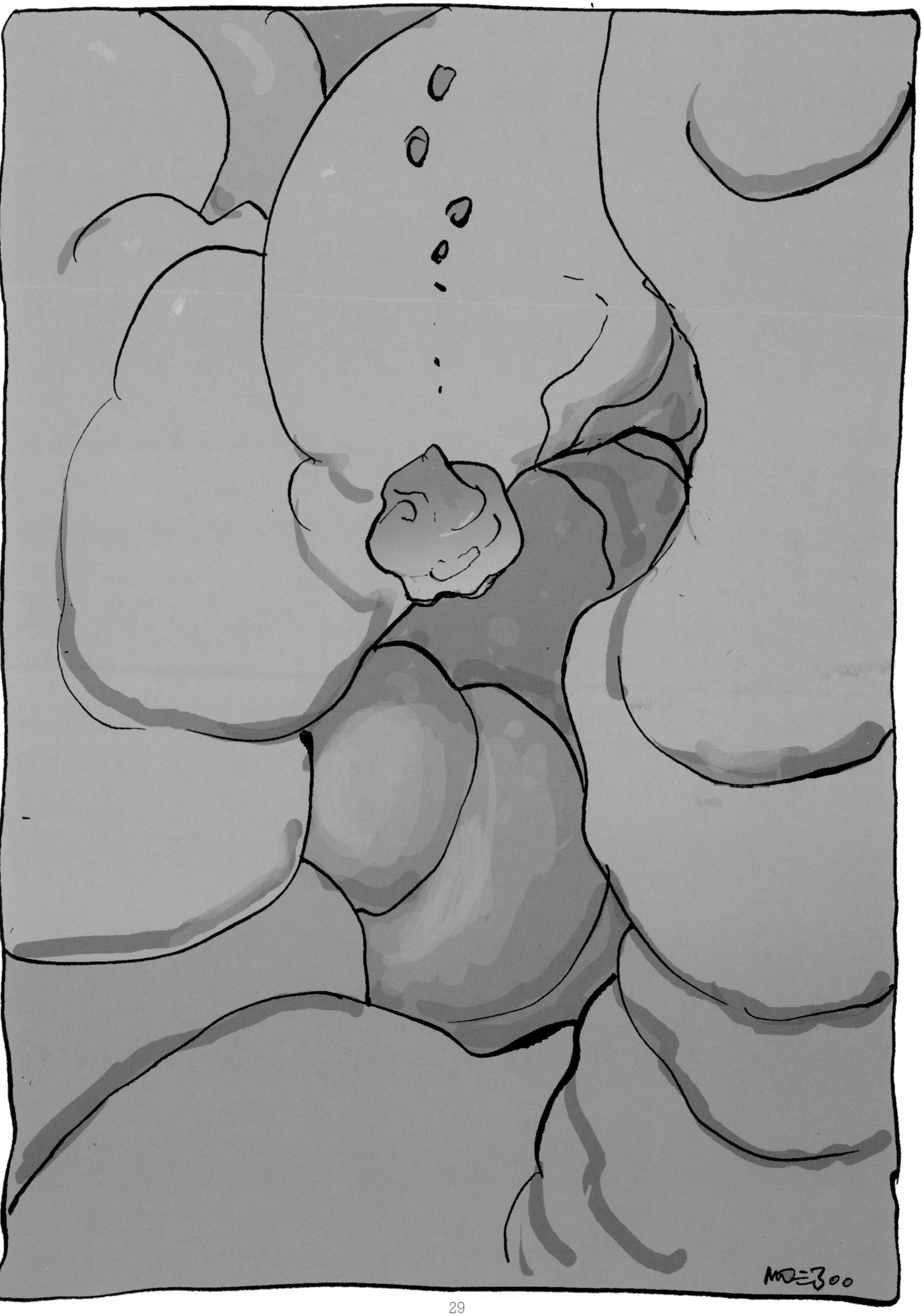

7
00
MOEBIUS

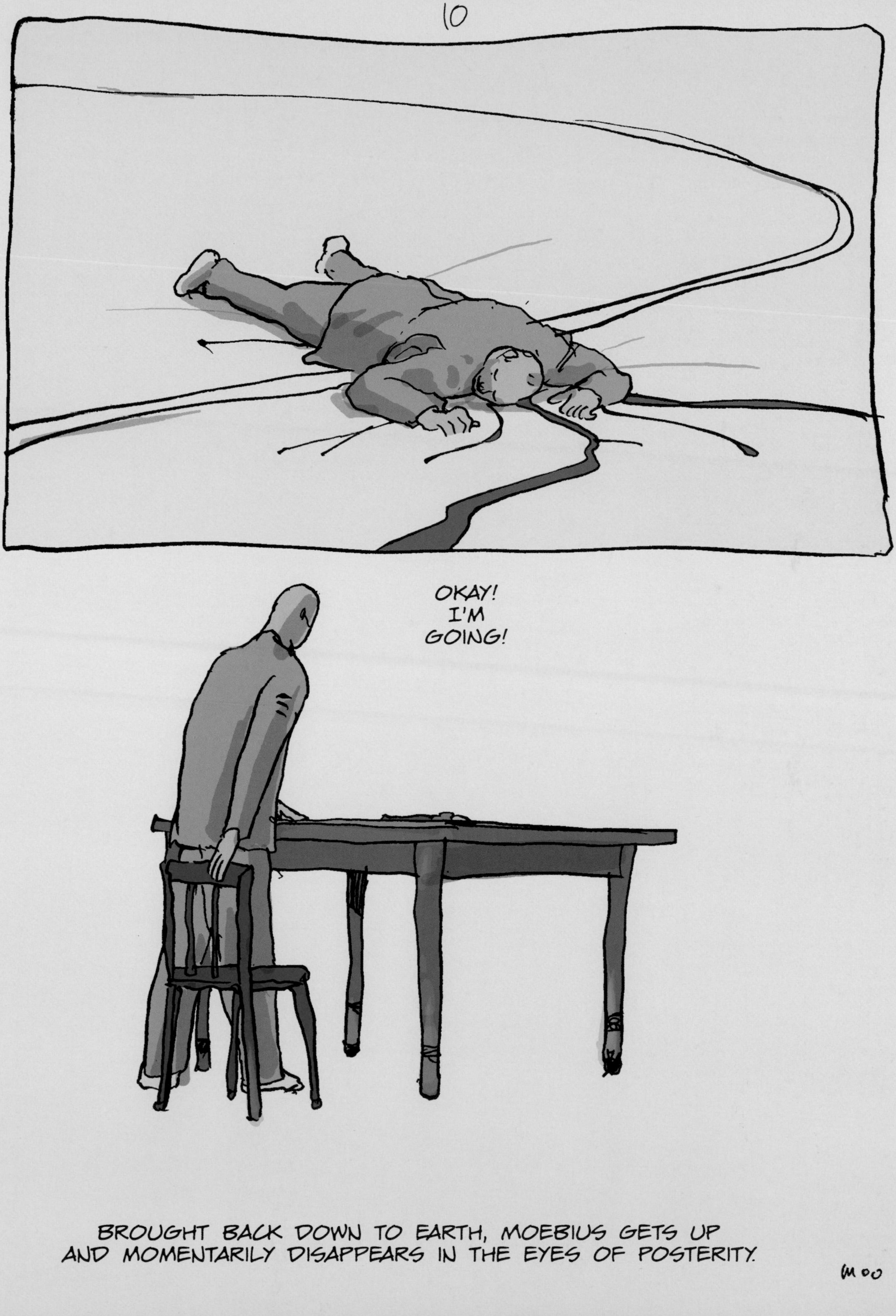

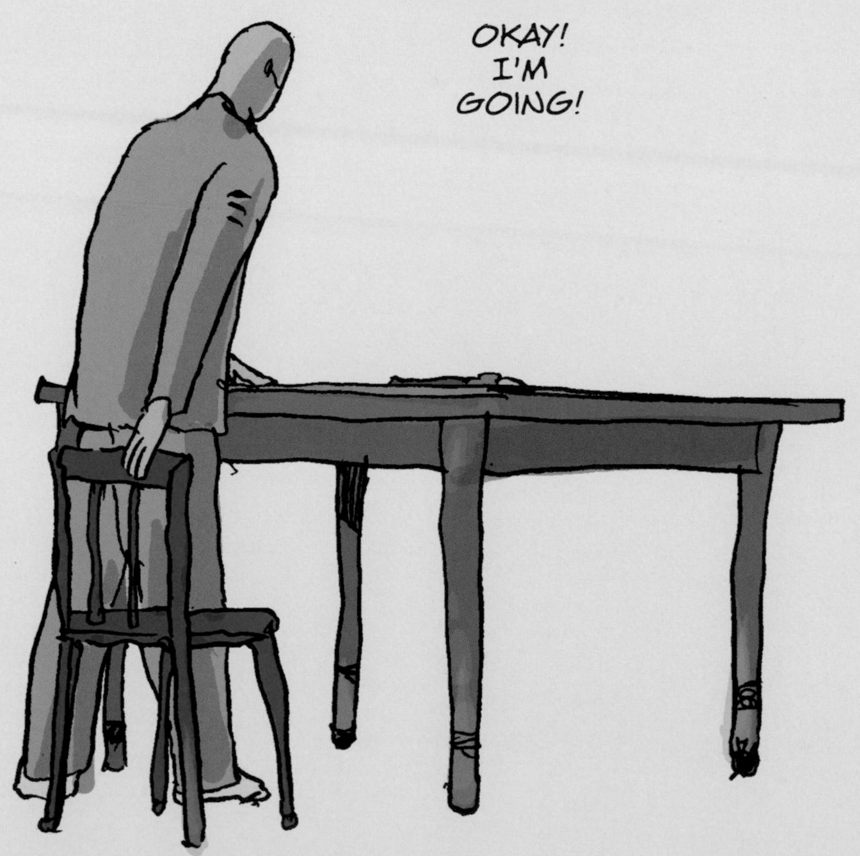

BROUGHT BACK DOWN TO EARTH, MOEBIUS GETS UP AND MOMENTARILY DISAPPEARS IN THE EYES OF POSTERITY.

HE DECIDES TO BEGIN
A **BLUEBERRY** SCRIPT.

I'M IN DEEP SHIT WITH THIS GERONIMO STORY.

...DUELS AT THE OK CORRAL! GOOD!

MOEB 01

"Smells like dead bodies again!"
"Nah, that's just the smell of Tombstone!"
"Ha ha! That's some nose you've got, Earp!"
"Gentlemen, a little quiet."
"Sherriff Earp claims to have proof that the Clantons and McLaurys are guilty."
"What about Geronimo...?"
"And what proof do we have?"
"This white spur found in the stagecoach.
"For me, that's the proof."
"Politically, Geronimo makes a better culprit."
"We'll have all the cowboys on our asses."
"I know."

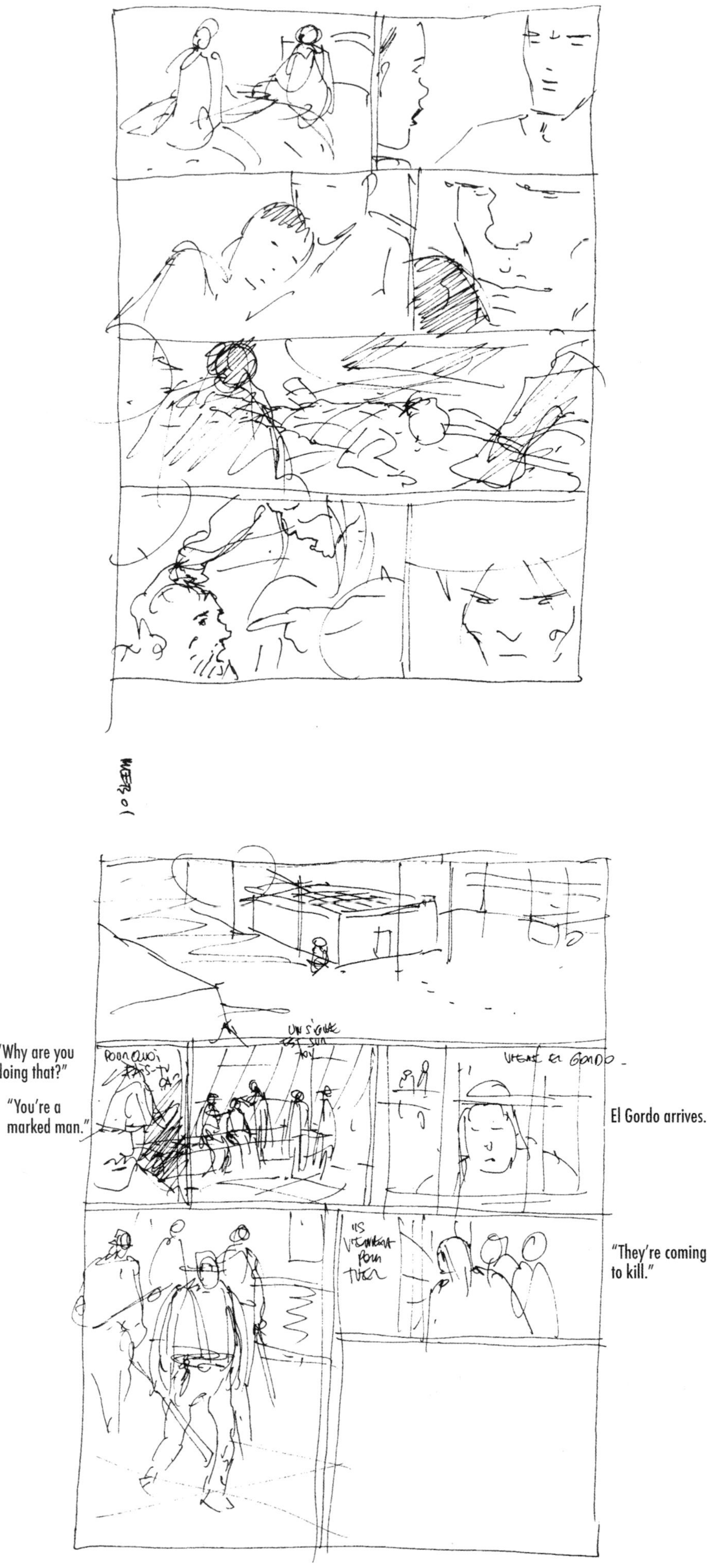
"Why are you doing that?"
"You're a marked man."
El Gordo arrives.
"They're coming to kill."

MOEB 01

MIERDA!...

IN PART THAT FELLOW CAN REALLY BE A PAIN.
IN PART, YES! BUT **WHICH** PART?
MOEBIUS 2001

SUDDENLY ...
BLOOD AND GUTS! SUDDENLY, I'M GETTING A FEW IDEAS...

17

INSTEAD OF WARNING EARP ABOUT THE TRAP...
CLUM TRIES TO CHARGE STRAWFIELD, BUT GETS HIMSELF CAUGHT AND THROWN TO THE BOTTOM OF THE SILVER MINE.
THROUGHOUT THE ENTIRE BOOK, CAMPBELL TRIES TO FIGURE OUT THE REST OF THE STORY, BUT HE DIES TOWARD THE END, WHISPERING, "WHAT HAPPENS...? I NEED TO KNOW WHAT HAPPENS!"
IN ANOTHER BOOK, BLUEBERRY WILL TELL THE END OF THE STORY TO PARKER, WHO IS SEEKING TRUE LOVE.

—CLUM MUST CHOOSE BETWEEN {GERONIMO → ARMY / EARP → OK CORRAL

(TO COME) KILLED BY THE KILLER

NOTHING!

NOTHING TO SMOKE AROUND HERE!

A REAL DESERT.
WAIT! SOME SORT OF BUNKER!
MŒB .01

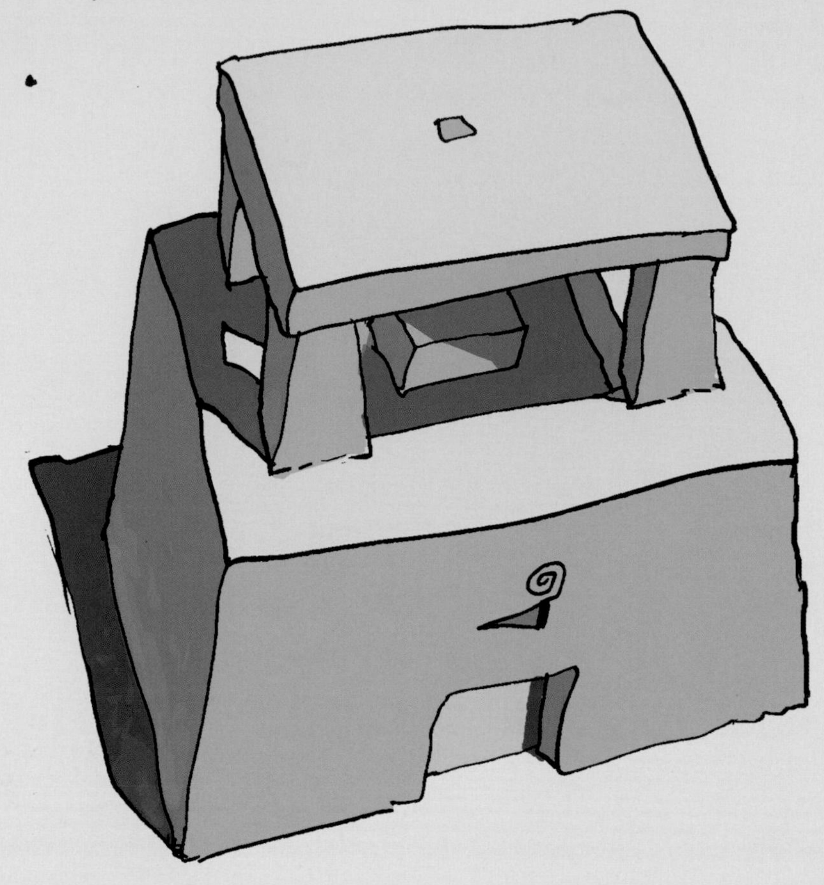
NOTHING
COULD EVER
MAKE ME GO
INSIDE A THING
LIKE THIS.

MOEBIUS TOMB RAIDER

YOU'D THINK THIS WAS A MOEBIUS COMIC...

...BUT NOT AS CLEVER!

HEY, I'M NOT LARA CROFT!

HERE'S THE BIT WITH THE DOOR
///

THE BIT WITH THE STAIRS...
HFF!

WAIT! THIS BIT'S NEW! A NAKED WOMAN!

COME.

WHAT FOR?

I HAVE A PRESENT FOR YOU...SOMETHING THAT YOU PARTICULARLY LIKE.

SO, IT'S A TRAP!

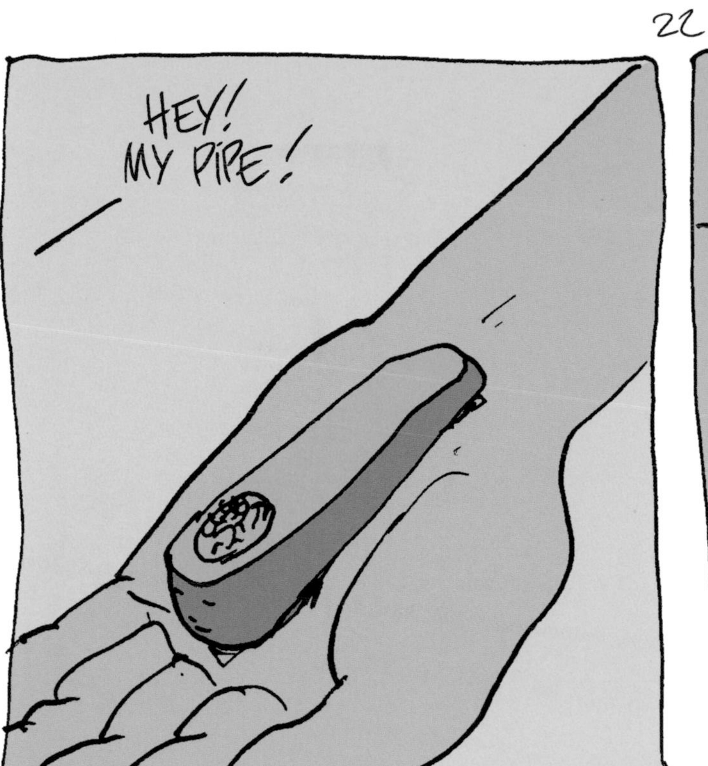
HEY!
MY PIPE!

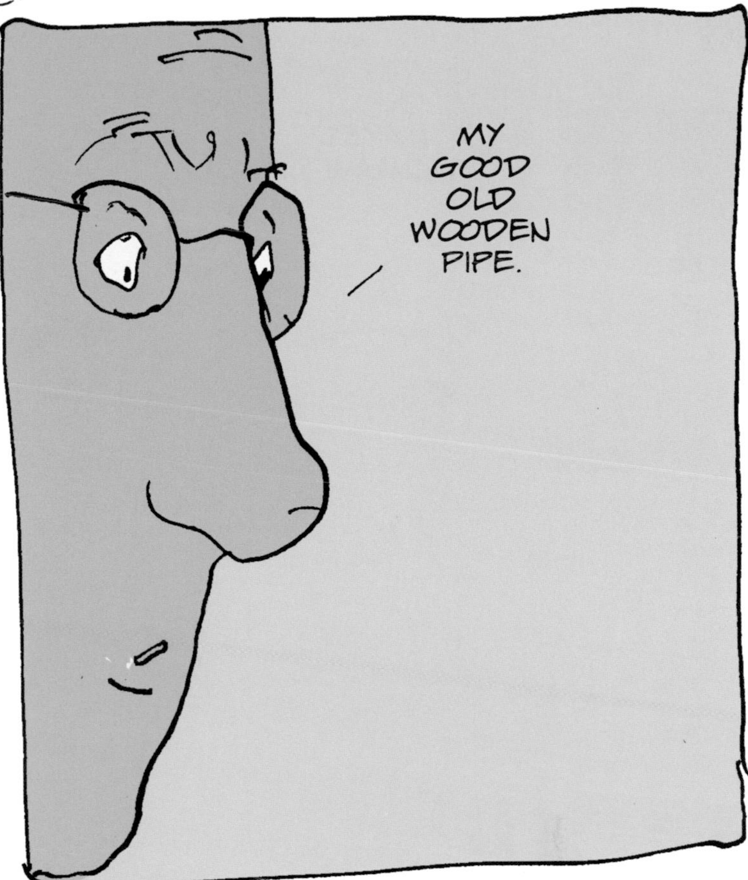
MY GOOD OLD WOODEN PIPE.

BUT... THERE'S SOME WEED PACKED IN IT!
GOOD WEED, TOO! ISN'T THAT WHAT YOU WANTED?

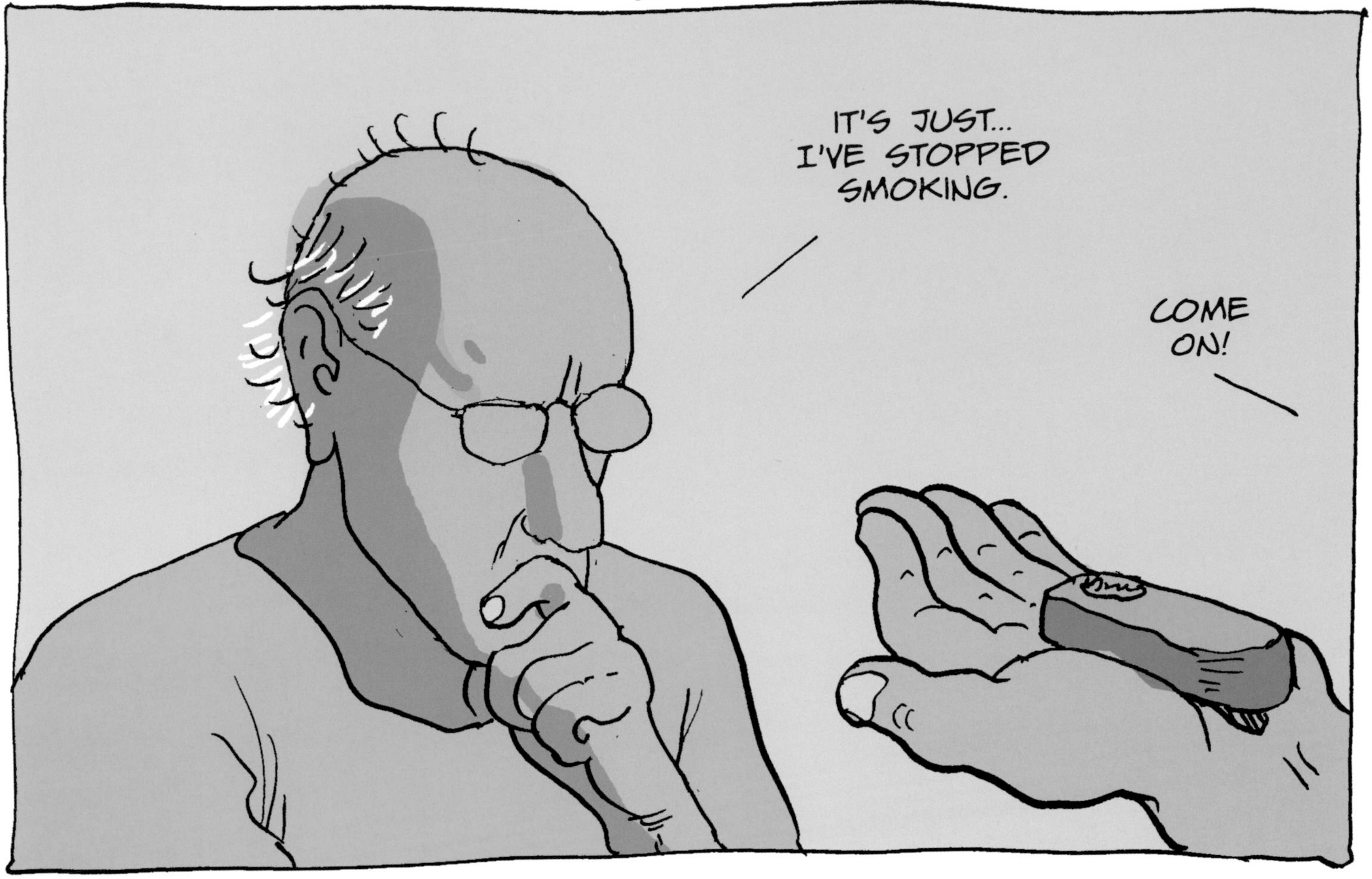

IT'S JUST...
I'VE STOPPED
SMOKING.

COME
ON!

AS I THOUGHT!

IT *IS*
A
TRAP.

WHAT
ARE YOU
AFRAID OF?
YOU'RE HERE--
IN YOUR OWN
DESERT!
YOU'RE AT
HOME.

MOEB 01

LATER...

GOOD GRIEF, I HELD OUT! I'M AS STRONG AS MATT SCUDDER.

ALL THE SAME...

...IT'S TRUE. THIS DESERT IS MINE.

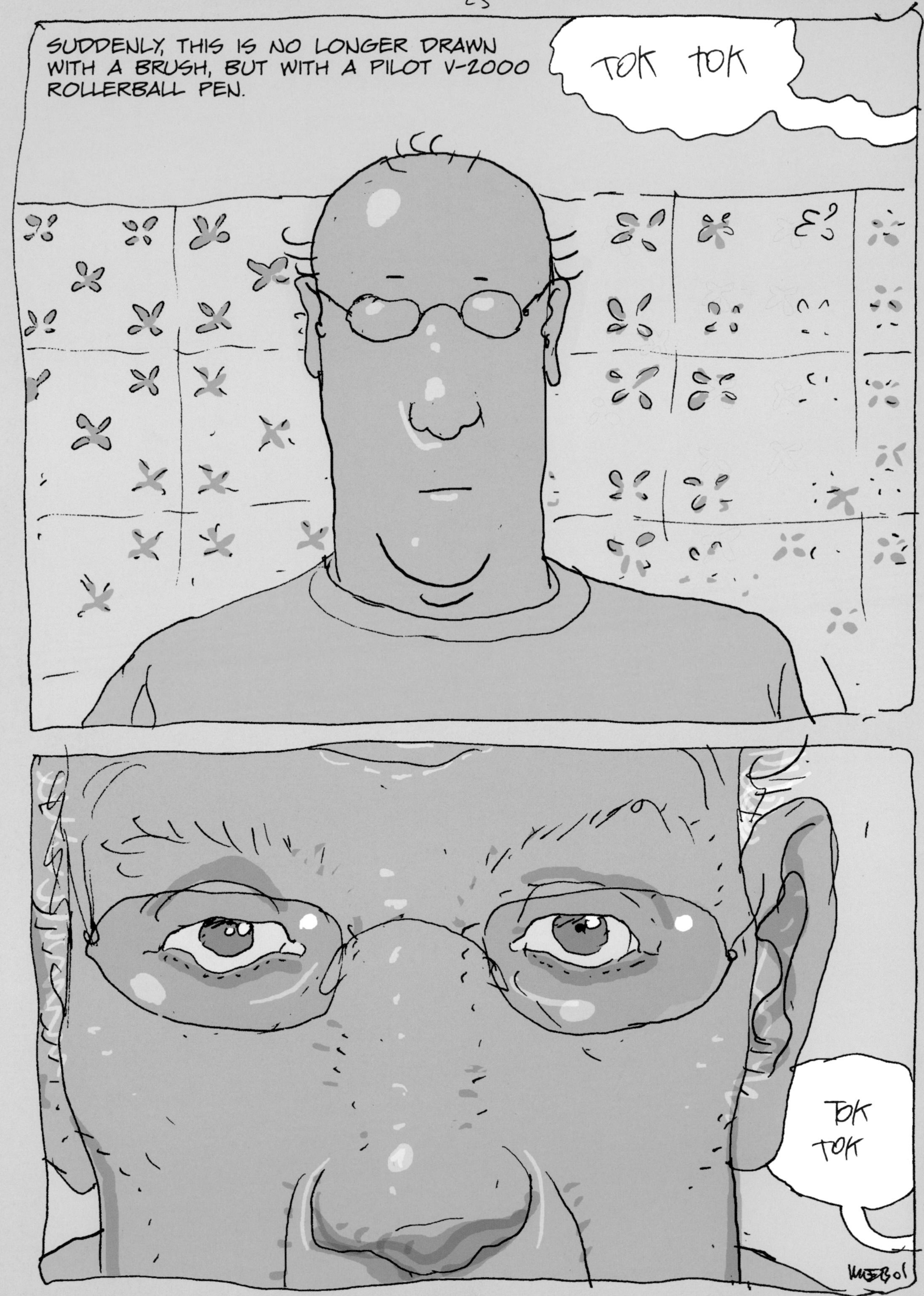
25
SUDDENLY, THIS IS NO LONGER DRAWN WITH A BRUSH, BUT WITH A PILOT V-2000 ROLLERBALL PEN.
TOK TOK
TOK TOK

COME IN.
TOK
TOK
COME IN, I SAID.
MOEBIUS
IT'S ME... ME.
UH... YES! YOU, ME!
IT'S BEEN AGES!
AGES! THAT'S IT! COME IN! I'VE BEEN WAITING FOR YOU!

IT'S INCREDIBLE, WHAT'S CHANGED...
YEAH, YEAH... SIT DOWN. WE NEED TO TALK, THE TWO OF US!
RIGHT!
MOEB
I MADE YOU COME BECAUSE THINGS ARE CHANGING PRETTY RAPIDLY.
AND HOW DOES THAT AFFECT **ME?** I'M NOT EVEN IN THE LOOP ANYMORE.

LET ME REMIND YOU THAT YOUR GRAPHIC NOVELS ARE STILL BEING PUBLISHED.
BUT... AREN'T **YOU** THE ONE WHO HOLDS THE RIGHTS?
TRUE! BUT THAT'S NOT THE THEME...
...OF THIS STORY.
THE THEME IS **WEED**. I'M DOING A SERIES OF STORIES ON DESERT "B"... DESERT "B" HERE, DESERT "B" THERE... THE READERS ARE WONDERING WHERE I'M GOING WITH THIS.
THAT'S NOTHING NEW.

AND IF YOU WANT MY ADVICE, IT'S BETTER TO LEAVE THEM IN THE DARK.
UH... I DON'T SEE WHAT'S SO ILL-ADVISED ABOUT--
WHOA... STOP!

C'MON... YOU'RE NOT REALLY GONNA SCOWL AT ME... AT ***ME?!***

THE HELL I WON'T!

LET ME REMIND YOU THAT YOU'RE THE ONE WHO BROUGHT ME HERE.

WRONG! YOU'RE THE ONE WHO BROUGHT ***ME*** HERE...

OKAY... IF YOU'RE TAKING ***THAT*** TACK, THEN CONVERSATION IS IMPOSSIBLE...

ZIP

HEY! YOU'RE NOT ***REALLY*** GOING TO SMOKE WEED IN HERE...

THE HELL I WON'T.

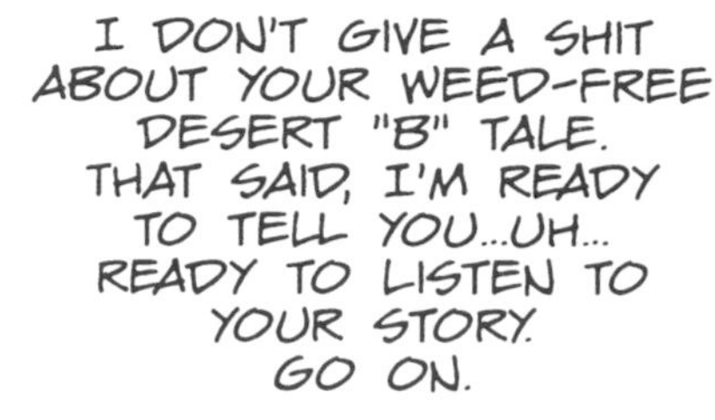
I DON'T GIVE A SHIT ABOUT YOUR WEED-FREE DESERT "B" TALE. THAT SAID, I'M READY TO TELL YOU...UH... READY TO LISTEN TO YOUR STORY. GO ON.

OKAY...AS I WAS SAYING... THE WORLD'S CHANGING...LOTS OF NEW AUTHORS ARE CROPPING UP... PEOPLE YOUR AGE, IF YOU GET WHAT I MEAN...
MM-HMM.

MARKET CONDITIONS ARE SHIFTING, EMPIRES COLLAPSING, IDOLS TEETERING, FEAR AND DEATH ARE ON THE PROWL...
HMMMMMMM.

HAAAPFFFF
TAP TIP TAP

PLEASE! SHIT OR GET OFF THE POT.

SNFF SNFF

VERY FUNNY.

I HAVE A PROBLEM WITH THE NEXT *BLUEBERRY*. THAT'S WHY I HAD YOU COME OVER. CAN YOU LOOK AT THIS?
A PROBLEM WITH THE SCRIPT OR WITH THE ART?
HMM... BOTH, HUH?
HM.
BOTH.
MŒBIUS 01

I'M WORRIED! THIS LOOKS LIKE FULL-BLOWN DEPRESSION IN THE END.

AND THE END CAN'T COME TOO SOON!

BUT WHAT ARE YOU IMPLYING?

SIMPLY THAT, FOR ONCE, HE'S VOICING IT DIRECTLY IN A STORY.

OH, AND YOU CALL THIS A **STORY?**

IT'S MOEBIUS !!! ...

PRECISELY MY POINT.

BANG!

MOEB 01

WHAT WAS THAT SOUND?
A DISCHARGE FROM A FIREARM, I SHOULD THINK.
IT CAME FROM THE OTHER SIDE OF THE "POT."
LET'S GO AROUND AND SEE WHAT'S UP.
IT'S STARTING AGAIN...
HEY! THIS IS AMAZING!
BANG! BANG!
BANG!
IT'S BLUEBERRY!
WHAT THE DEVIL IS HE DOING HERE?
MŒB 01

NO...I STILL PREFER LEMON TO VINEGAR IN A SALAD.

YOU AND YOUR SALADS!

NM!
MYAMM!
SLURP!
GLUP!
CRUNCH!
MMGHM!

AHHH... THAT'S BETTER!

DON'T **YOU** FEEL BETTER, TOO?

BLUEBERRY! **SAY** SOMETHING, OLD BOY!

MOEBIUS 01

BLOOD AND GUTS, THAT'S ENOUGH!!!
?
?
BAG THIS LAME STORY RIGHT NOW AND GET BUSY WITH MY SCRIPT! OTHERWISE I'M PLANTIN' SIX BULLETS IN YOUR NOGGIN. I AIN'T KIDDIN', YA DIRTY COYOTE!
HE'S RIGHT! I'VE GOTTEN MYSELF INTO A FINE MESS.
HERE...HAVE A TOKE INSTEAD.
CALM DOWN!
YOU'RE NOT GOING TO MAKE A SCENE OVER A STORY SCENE, ARE YOU?
GRR!
KLIK KLAK
MOEB01

NO WAY! I'VE STOPPED!
WHAT?
HUH?
AGAIN?
Y'ALL KNOW! THIS AIN'T THE FIRST TIME HE'S QUIT!
HEY! WAIT... WHAT'S HE DOING?
THAT'S OUTTA LINE!
BLUEBERRY DOES NOT GET HIGH! YOU DIG?
MŒB01

TWO THINGS... WE HAVE TO STICK TO LOCAL CUSTOMS! YOU KNOW IT... BLUEBERRY CAN DRINK HIMSELF TO **DEATH,** BUT THERE'S NO WAY HE CAN TOUCH WEED, OPIUM, PEYOTE, OR ANY OTHER SHIT...OKAY?

OKAY!

OKAY!

OKAY!

SECOND... BLUEBERRY, ARZAK, MAJOR, ALL OF YOU... GO AHEAD AND DO WHATEVER YOU WANT. BUT **OUTSIDE** THE STORY...OUTSIDE **ALL** THE STORIES, OKAY?

WELL.

WE'LL SEE.

PFFT!

MOEB. 01

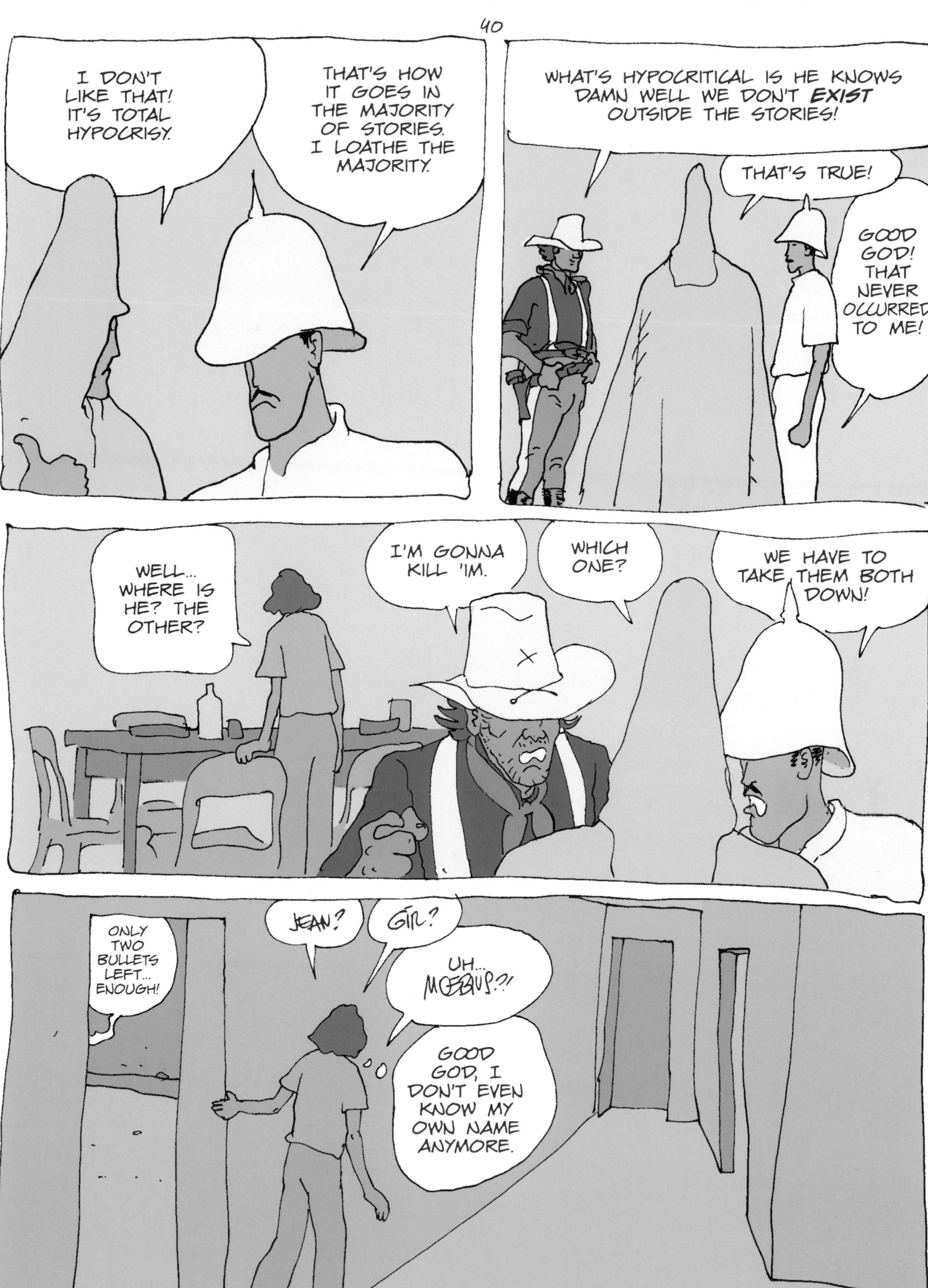
I DON'T LIKE THAT! IT'S TOTAL HYPOCRISY.
THAT'S HOW IT GOES IN THE MAJORITY OF STORIES. I LOATHE THE MAJORITY.
WHAT'S HYPOCRITICAL IS HE KNOWS DAMN WELL WE DON'T **EXIST** OUTSIDE THE STORIES!
THAT'S TRUE!
GOOD GOD! THAT NEVER OCCURRED TO ME!
WELL... WHERE IS HE? THE OTHER?
I'M GONNA KILL 'IM.
WHICH ONE?
WE HAVE TO TAKE THEM BOTH DOWN!
ONLY TWO BULLETS LEFT... ENOUGH!
JEAN?
GIR?
UH... MOEBIUS?!
GOOD GOD, I DON'T EVEN KNOW MY OWN NAME ANYMORE.
MOEB 91

I'M OUT! FINALLY!
I WAS GETTING SICK OF LISTENING TO ALL THAT BICKERING.
I NEED TO TAKE OFF, THAT'S FOR SURE! BUT WHICH WAY?

I'M WORRIED ABOUT HIM!
ARWATCHER
HE'S LOST HIS HAIR! I'M SURE THOSE TEETH ARE FALSE! AND HE'S GROWN A POTBELLY!
OH! THERE'S THE DOOR.
NICE SHOOTING! BLUEBERRY HASN'T LOST HIS TOUCH...
GOOD GRIEF! THAT REMINDS ME OF SOME-THING.
I ABSOLUTELY NEED TO TALK TO HIM BEFORE IT'S TOO LATE.
WHERE IS HE?

THIS IS MY DESERT! **MY** DESERT "B"!

MŒB 01

ARZAK! THE MAJOR! AND BLUEBERRY! THEY'RE ALL AGAINST ME.
ONLY JOHN DiFOOL HAS LEFT ME ALONE.
I HOPE HE DOESN'T HAVE IT IN FOR JODOROWSKY...
HUP HUP!
GOOD GRIEF! NO DICE. HE ONLY KNOWS HIS MASTER.
HA! THERE'S WHAT I NEED!
WILL YOU COME DOWN?
CROOT!

I CAN'T STAND IT!

THE CREATURES DON'T RECOGNIZE ME! MAYBE I'VE CHANGED TOO MUCH.

STILL, I CAN'T LEAVE **MYSELF** IN THAT STATE...

ON TOP OF THAT, HE'S CAPABLE OF ANYTHING! EVEN PUBLISHING THIS STORY...NO MATTER WHERE... WITH STARDOM OR WITH L'ASSOCIATION. HE'S HEADING FOR BIG TROUBLE... WORSE THAN DIDIANO!*

* INTENSE PHOTOGRAPHER.

ANYONE HOME?
8

WHAT DO YOU WANT?
?!!
8

I'M IN SEARCH OF... THE AUTHOR.
DON'T TELL ME ANY TALL TALES! YOU ARE THE AUTHOR.
THAT'S NOT VERY CLEAR... I DON'T ANSWER THAT KIND OF QUESTION... EVER.
IN THE PAST IT WAS ME... NOW, IN THE PRESENT, IT'S NO LONGER ME, BUT ME IN THE FUTURE... WHICH IS TO SAY, NOT YET ME...
WELL... WHAT KIND OF QUESTION DO YOU ANSWER?
QUESTIONS LIKE, "WHERE IS GOD?" "WHAT DOES HE DO?" AND SO ON.
8
OH, OKAY! THAT KIND OF QUESTION?
LET'S SEE...
WE'LL START FROM THE PREMISE THAT GOD IS THE CREATOR...ALL RIGHT?
UH... ALL RIGHT. SO FAR, SO GOOD!
OKAYYY...
8
NOW THE QUESTION BECOMES... WHO MADE YOU?

47

I SEE EXACTLY WHERE YOU'RE GOING WITH THIS. IF THE AUTHOR MADE US, THEN HE'S LIKE GOD FOR US...SO QUESTIONS CONCERNING HIM CONCERN ME...
THAT'S IT.
THAT SAID, HOW SHOULD I CONSIDER **YOU?** AS A CREATURE CREATED BY DESIGN OR AS A... UH...AS GOD HIMSELF?
UH.
WELL...JUST CALL ME GOD...
HEH HEH HEH!
HAHAHA!
OKAY!
GOOD... SO, **WHAT'S** YOUR QUESTION?
HEE HEE!

I WANT TO SPEAK TO THE AUTHOR.
BADLY PHRASED...
OH, SHIT! I WANT TO SPEAK TO GOD!
THERE YOU GO! DON'T BE SHY!
YOU WANT TO SPEAK TO YOUR FUTURE SELF, THEN?
YES-- AND RIGHT NOW!
WHAT ARE YOU DOING? STOP SHAKING MY CRATE!
I'M FED UP.
WAIT! DON'T LEAVE, IN THE NAME OF GOD!
MŒBIUS

I'VE BECOME TOO COMPLICATED.
I HAVE SOMETHING TO SAY.
WHERE'S GOD? WHERE IS **GOD?**
I WAS SIMPLER BEFORE.
MB 01

BEFORE...
WHEN I GROW UP, I'M GONNA TREAT MYSELF TO ONE-HUNDRED-POUND BAGS OF MARBLES!
YOUR TURN, JEANNOT!
•RUE PASTEUR, FONTENAY-SOUS-BOIS, FRANCE, 1951.
WOLINSKI 01

GOOD GRIEF! WHO'S THE GUY WALKING UP TO THEM? HE LOOKS--NO!
NO DOUBT ABOUT IT! IT'S ME!
UH... HIM!
BUT...
...WHAT'S HE DOING?
OH, MY! I'M HALLUCINATING!
UH... THANKS, MISTER.
100 lbs
IT'S THAT FUCKING WEED! IT'S TOO POTENT.
WEB 01

DON'T BOTHER HIDING! I KNOW YOU'RE THERE.

SO... YOU HAVE SOMETHING TO SAY?
YEAH... WHAT YOU DID TO THAT KID IS GROSS, BUT... OKAY!
THAT'S NOT THE PROBLEM!

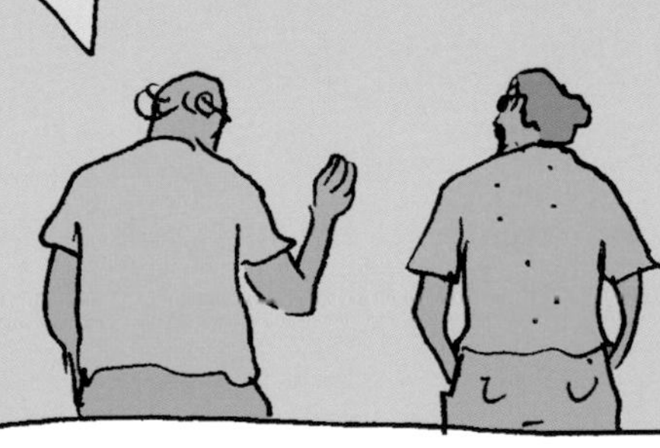
I KNOW WHAT YOU'RE GOING TO SAY! I REALLY FUCKED UP WITH BLUEBERRY.
I DON'T UNDERSTAND YOU... HOW COULD YOU DO SOMETHING SO STUPID? JEAN-MICHEL WILL BE ALL OVER YOUR ASS.

WAIT...YOU DON'T KNOW?
KNOW WHAT ?

WELL, JEAN-MICHEL DIED IN 1990...
NO!
MOEB 01

SHIT, MAN... THAT HIT ME HARD! HAS ANYONE ELSE DIED?
WELL... NOT YET...
TELL ME ABOUT THE FUTURE. HOW'S IT GOING IN YOUR TIME?
PFFT! CHIRAC'S THE PRESIDENT.
WE HAD MITTERRAND FOR FOURTEEN YEARS.
I KNEW ABOUT MITTERRAND. I GO RIGHT UP TO THE MID-EIGHTIES.
WELL...MAINLY, THERE WAS THE FALL OF THE BERLIN WALL AND THE ATTACK ON NEW YORK.
ATTACK ON NEW YORK?!
YOU KNOW, THE WORLD TRADE CENTER. TERRORISTS HIJACKED TWO BOEINGS FILLED WITH PASSENGERS AND FLEW THEM INTO THE TWIN TOWERS.
THE TOWERS COLLAPSED IN FLAMES, KILLING THOUSANDS OF PEOPLE...THEN A THIRD BIRD CRASHED INTO THE PENTAGON... I DON'T HAVE TO TELL YOU HOW FEATHERS WENT FLYING EVERYWHERE...
SHIT...
THAT REALLY THREW ME FOR A LOOP, AS IF WE WERE SUDDENLY ON ANOTHER PLANET...
AND... WHO DID THIS HORRIFIC THING? THE ARABS?

NOT REALLY... A GROUP OF ISLAMISTS, IN FACT!
AND WHAT HAPPENED AFTERWARDS ?
AFTER?
I DUNNO...IT'S 2001 RIGHT NOW, AND THAT OCCURRED JUST A FEW DAYS AGO. I CAN TELL YOU ABOUT YOUR FUTURE, BUT NOT MINE.
ANYWAY, I'M SHOOK UP!
SHIT! YOUR STORY BEATS ALL SCIENCE FICTION.
WELL, ABOUT BLUEBERRY...BE CAREFUL. THERE MUST BE RIGHTS HOLDERS TO KEEP EVERYTHING ON THE UP-AND-UP.
YEAH...THERE'S CHRISTINE...
CHRISTINE IS COOL.
SUPER COOL! BUT IT'S JEAN-MICHEL'S SON WHO OVERSEES IT ALL.
WAIT! JEAN-MICHEL'S **SON?** LITTLE PHILIPPE? HOLD ON... ***I'LL*** GO TELL THAT KID A THING OR TWO!

STOP! DON'T FORGET HE'S ALL GROWN UP! YOU WANNA GET ME KILLED, OR WHAT?
NO!
YES! AND...
SHIT, MAN. I CAN'T **BELIEVE** THAT.
I'LL GO--
NO! SHH!
SHIT.
YEAH... SHIT!
MOE 01

57

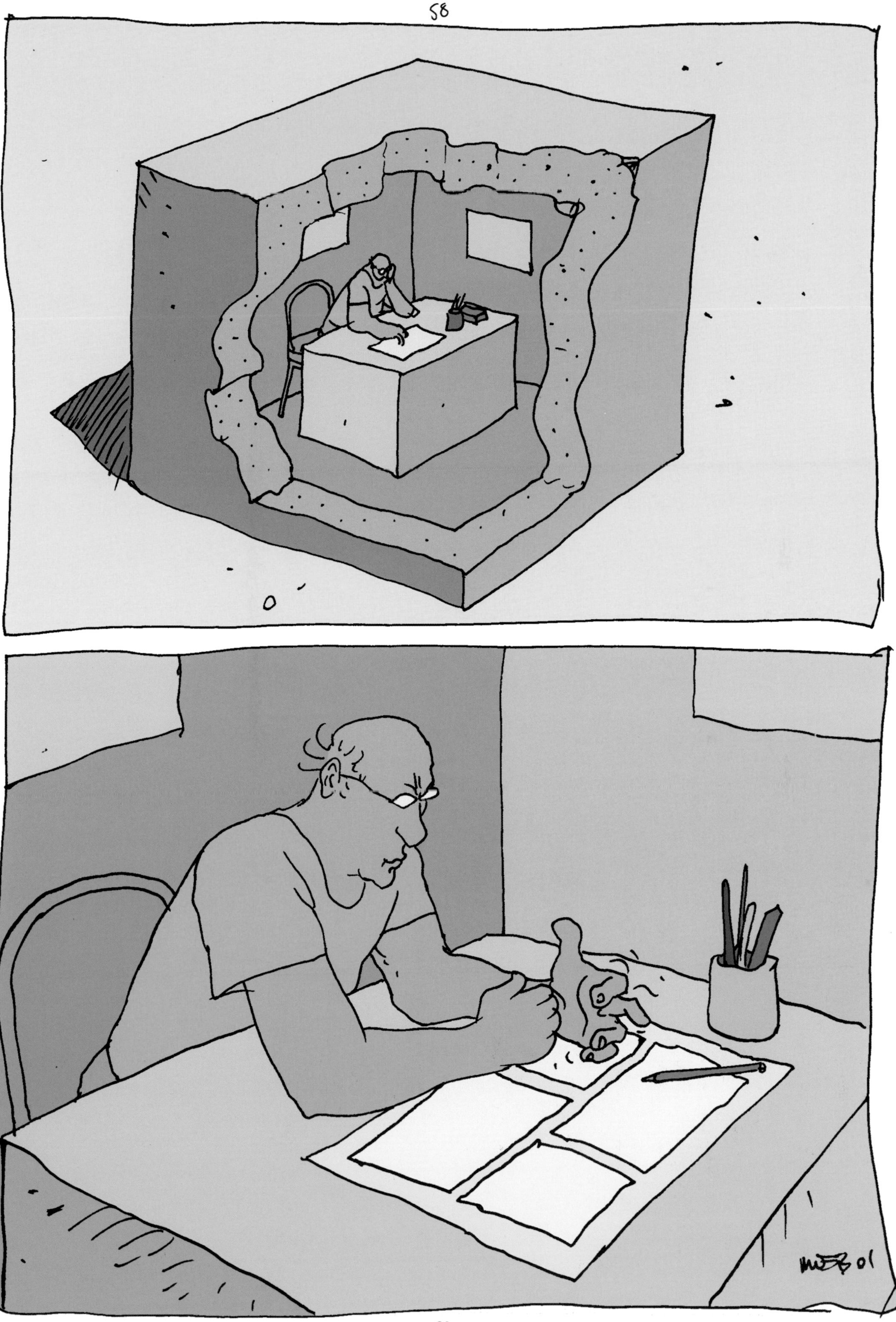

HOW LONG'S HE BEEN INSIDE NOW?

TIME DOESN'T EXIST IN COMICS... PANELS ARE USED INSTEAD...

OKAY, THEN...HE'S BEEN INSIDE THAT CUBE FOR HOW MANY PANELS?

FORTY-FIVE PANELS, DEPENDING ON HOW YOU COUNT THEM.

THE REAL QUESTION IS...

...WHAT IS HE **DOING** INSIDE?

60
C'MON, HOW DO YOU DRAW HANDS ALREADY?
MŒB

STOP DRAWIN
THIS STORY
IMMEDIATELY.
WHAT
I DON'T
UNDE
I'D BET HE'S DRAWING. IN ANY CASE, THAT'S ALL HE KNOWS HOW TO DO.
IT'S AN OBSESSION WITH HIM.
HEY! WHAT ARE YOU TWO DOIN'?
?
OH, NOOO! NOT HIM!

HRM! WE WERE GIVEN STRICT ORDERS! YOU ARE NOT TO APPEAR **ANYMORE!** IN FACT, YOU'RE TO ***DIS***APPEAR!

BUT--

IT'S TOO DANGEROUS WHEN YOU'RE AROUND!

DISAPPEAR RIGHT AWAY, MIKE! YOU'RE TOO RISKY. THE ONLY SWEARING YOU'RE ALLOWED IS: (1) "BLOODY HELL!" AND (2) "BLOOD AND GUTS!" ANY DEVIATION PUTS US ALL IN DANGER...
SHIT!
MŒB 01

ON TO NEW ADVENTURES IN THE LAND OF OUR FOREFATHERS!
AH! THERE'S THE MAJOR!
TAKE ME TO YOUR MASTE
HE'S NOT HERE.
WHAT DO YOU WANT?
STOP DRAWING THIS STORY IMMEDIATELY.
WHAT? I DON'T UNDER-STAND.

I WONDER IF THIS NEW COMIC WILL BE A HIT.

I'LL SHOW IT TO MY EDITOR.

IN ANY CASE, IT'S PURE MOEBIUS.

TOK TOK

MOEB 01

70
?
ANYONE HOME?
WHAT DO YOU WANT?
I'M IN SEARCH OF... THE AUTHOR.
WHAT DO YOU WANT FROM THE AUTHOR?

HMM... IT'S JUST THAT... I...UH... I'LL SEE WHAT I CAN DO.

THANKS... FOR HIS SAKE.

IN THE MEANTIME, I'M PLUGGING THIS HOLE!
I'M SICK OF JUST ANYONE SHOWING UP WITH THEIR IDIOTIC QUESTIONS!
?

STOP DRAWING THIS STORY IMMEDIATELY.
!!!

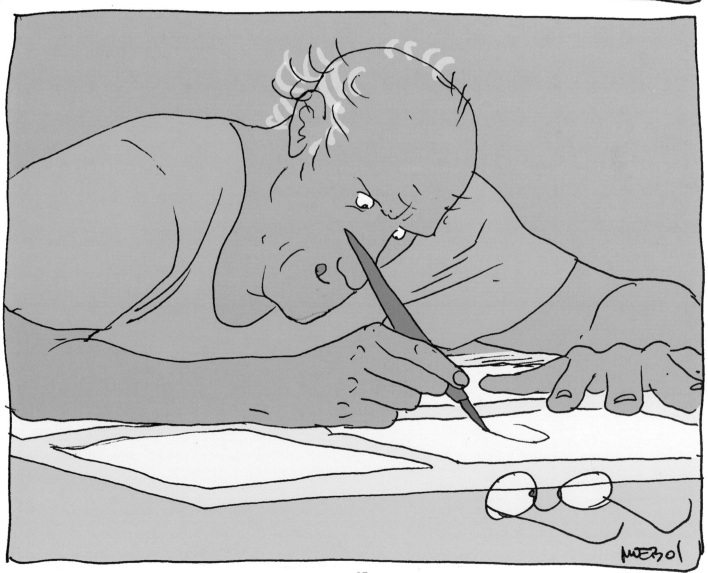

DESSIN DE GIR
SCENARIO DE ~~MOEBIUS~~ ~~GIR~~ ~~PATRICK CAUVIN~~ KLOTZ

HRFP!
THAT'S THE BEST I CAN DO...
ENOUGH FOR TODAY!
I'M BEAT!

76

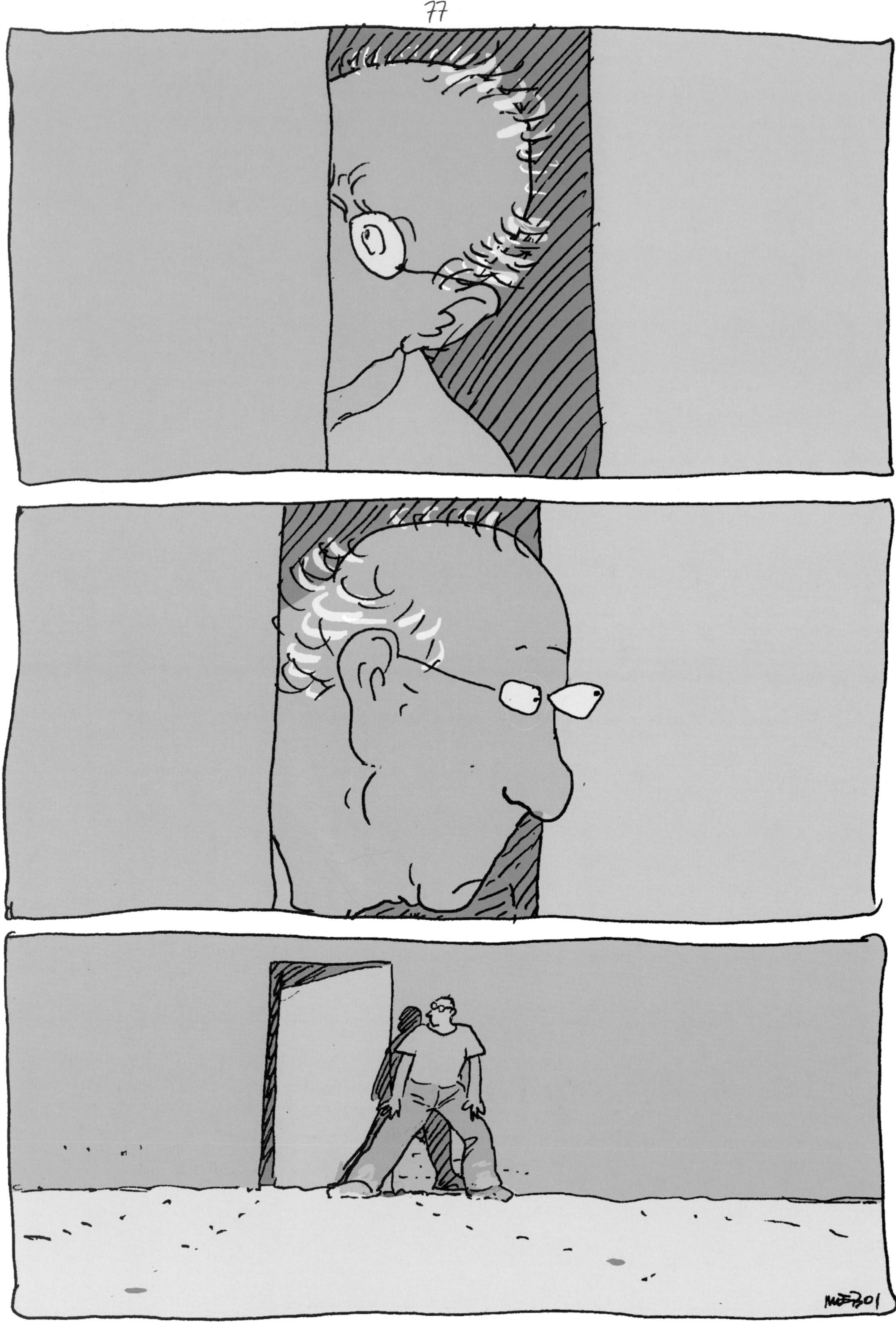

LATER...
FINALLY! ALONE IN DESERT "B"...
MOEBIUS 01

MŒB 01

83

TO BE CONTINUED...

M.01

FUMETTI (II)

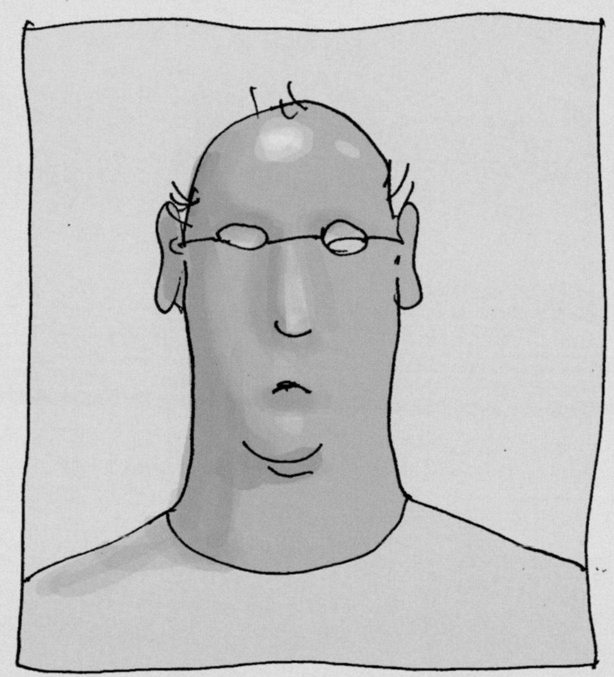

MOEBIUS
2001

INSIDE MOEBIUS

VOLUME 2

Arzak represents
the otherworldly perspective!
Absolutely indispensable for
understanding human behavior!

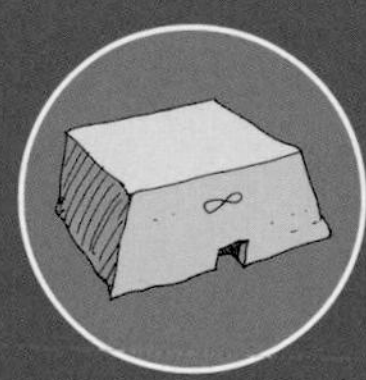

2
MŒBO6

FUMETTI!

2
THOSE ARE THE TOWERS OF THE WORLD...
...TRADE CENTER THAT ARE BURNING.
SO SAD.
I WONDER... WHO COULD HAVE **DONE** SOMETHING LIKE THAT...?
IT WAS ME, SAHIB.
MŒB 01

???
OHHH...
I DIDN'T SEE
YOU COMING.
THIS
DOES
NOT
SURPRISE
ME.
WHO...WHO
ARE YOU?
OSAMA!
OSAMA
BIN
LADEN!
MOE 01

I WAS SHOCKED AT FIRST, BUT AFTER ALL--SINCE DESERT "B" IS MINE--ANYTHING CAN HAPPEN.
IT IS TRUE THAT, AT THE MOMENT, I WILL NOT SURFACE IN JUST ANY PLACE. YOU KNOW THERE IS A PRICE ON MY HEAD.
I KNOW...BUT TELL ME, WHAT EXACTLY DO YOU WANT FROM ME?
FIRST, I SHOULD LIKE TO SAY SOMETHING IMPORTANT: MAN IS A MYSTERY.
MAN IS A MYSTERY...HMM...
AGREED!
BUT ALL OF IT'S A MYSTERY! MAN, ANIMALS, PLANTS, THE EARTH, THE SOLAR SYSTEM...
...THE GALAXY, STAR CLUSTERS, SUPERCLUSTERS, THE UNIVERSE... GOD, ME, LANGUAGE, LINES ON PAPER...
ALL.

HM.
THEN WE ARE IN UNISON! DO NOT OVEREXCITE YOURSELF! ALLOW ME TO POUR YOU SOME TEA.
THANK YOU... AND FORGIVE ME. I GOT CARRIED AWAY! LOOK, THERE'S THE MAJOR. I THINK THIS CONVERSATION WILL INTEREST HIM.
SO, MAJOR...? WHAT DO YOU SAY?
I'D SAY THIS IS DEUCEDLY AWKWARD...
AWKWARD?
MŒBIUS 01

6

MY DEAR MOEB, I KNOW THAT THIS PLACE BELONGS TO YOU...AND THAT THE CHOICE OF GUESTS IS ENTIRELY YOUR BAILIWICK...
...BUT I MUST NONETHELESS REMIND YOU THAT THIS MAN IS A CRIMINAL, WITH THE DEATHS OF MANY INNOCENT THOUSANDS ON HIS CONSCIENCE.
INNOCENT?
ARE THE DEMONS OF HELL INNOCENT? THEY SERVE EVIL WITH SUCH FERVOR THAT THEY FORGET THE HEINOUS NATURE OF THEIR WORK.
BUT --
IF YOU WOULD ...
...BEFORE WE CONTINUE THIS DISCUSSION, I WOULD LIKE TO PERFORM A SMALL RITUAL, A **MUST** IN MY CULTURE.
?
?

7
WAIT, WHAT'S HE DOING?
DO STIFLE THE IDIOTIC QUESTIONS!
BUT... BUT I...
ONE MOMENT... DAMN CELLPHONE...
DOODLE-OOOO
DOODLE-OOOO
YES?
IT IS NOT SERIOUS!
HMM.
NO! SELL! I SAID, SELL!
HEY.
FWWWT....
HEY, WAIT!
THIS HAS TO BE A DREAM.
THE GUY INTRUDES UPON MY DESERT AND ROLLS UP A JOINT RIGHT IN FRONT OF ME!
AND NOT ONLY DOES HE ROLL IT, BUT HE'S SMOKING IT!
PFFFFFF...
KOF KOF
MAJOR...? A TOKE?
OH, NO!
TA, BUT IT'S MIXED WITH TOBACCO... AND I PREFER NOT.
MOEBIUS

YOU, THE AUTHOR...I SHALL NOT OFFER YOU ANY. I KNOW YOU HAVE QUIT, BUT YOU MAKE A BIG MISTAKE...

IT IS AFGHANI!
THE BEST!

TO RESUME...MAJOR, YOUR SCRUPLES ARE BUT THE PRODUCT OF YOUR SOCIETY'S MORAL DECADENCE.
REALLY! I'VE HEARD THIS A HUNDRED TIMES.
YES, THAT MORAL DECADENCE BIT...EVEN I EXPECTED BETTER!

YOUR JUDEO-CHRISTIAN RELIGION INVENTED THE CONCEPT OF GUILT... AN EFFECTIVE SPIRITUAL TOOL, BUT VERY DESTRUCTIVE IN THE LONG RUN. IN OUR CULTURE, IT BARELY EXISTS.

WE HAVE ALWAYS PREFERRED SHAME.
SHAME?
YES... SHAME!
WHOA!

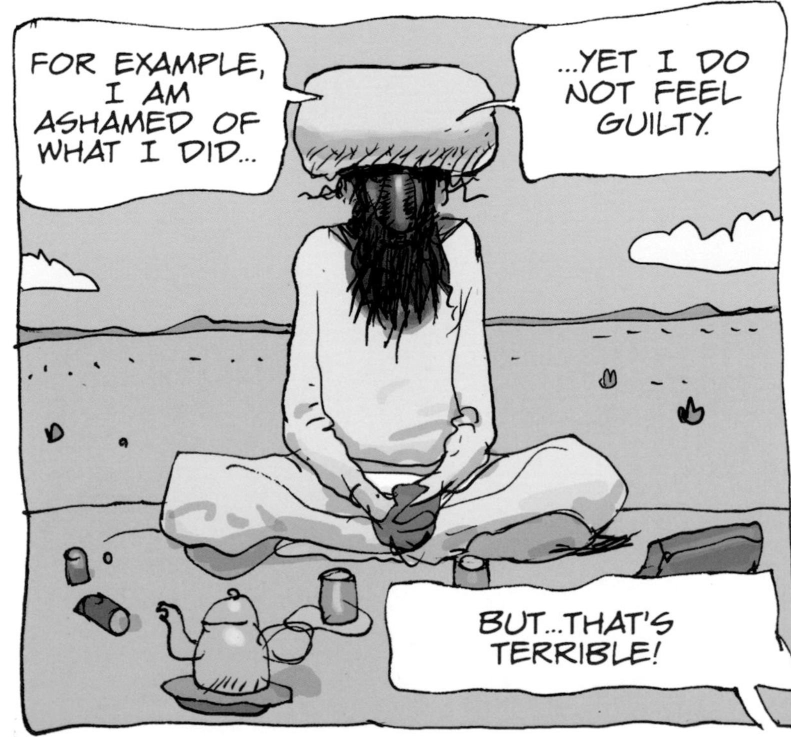

FOR EXAMPLE, I AM ASHAMED OF WHAT I DID...
...YET I DO NOT FEEL GUILTY.
BUT...THAT'S TERRIBLE!

I'LL ADMIT...I DON'T UNDERSTAND.
I DO.
?
!!!

IT'S THAT ONE AGAIN!
DON'T BLAME MISTER "B"...I CAME OF MY OWN FREE WILL.
WOW, IT'S GERONIMO!

BEFORE ALL ELSE...
...ALLOW ME TO PAY MY RESPECTS. I ADMIRE EVERYTHING YOU'VE DONE!
!?
IT IS MY HONOR TO SHAKE THE HAND OF A TRUE FORERUNNER.

YOU WOULD LIKE?
GLADLY...

KOF
BEURK
KOF

WHAT'S THIS NASTY SHIT? NOT ONLY DOES IT CONTAIN TOBACCO, BUT IT'S NOT EVEN WEED.
HO, MY BROTHER, IT IS AFGHANI SHIT! YOU WILL FLY HIGH--RIGHT TO HEAVEN.
SPEAKING OF, MOEB... WHERE ARE YOU TAKING US?
GOOD QUESTION.
TRUE THAT! WHERE?

UM...
MOEB 01

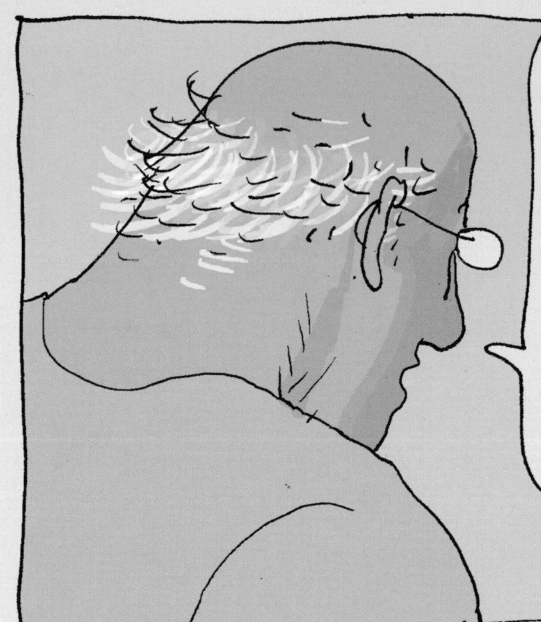
I...UH...I DON'T HAVE ANY IDEA... AND I'D LIKE TO POINT OUT THAT I'M IN THE SAME POSITION YOU ARE...SURE, I'M THE AUTHOR'S ICON AND HIS SPOKESMAN, BUT HE'S THE ONE CONTROLLING EVERYTHING HERE... DON'T ASK ME WHERE WE'RE HEADING...HE'S THE GAMEMASTER...
I MYSELF DO NOT AGREE.

I REPEAT-- I'M HERE OF MY OWN FREE WILL! NO ONE HAS EVER BEEN ABLE TO CONTROL ME IN MY ENTIRE LIFE, AND I'M NOT ABOUT TO CAVE NOW. ESPECIALLY TO A PALEFACE WHO'S GLUED TO HIS DRAWING BOARD... I'M HERE TO SUPPORT MY PAL BIN... I COMPLETELY APPROVE OF WHAT HE DID. IN HIS PLACE, I'D HAVE SENT A THOUSAND BOEINGS, NOT JUST THREE! HUH! I SAID IT.

GERONIMO IS CORRECT. HE IS MASTER TO US ALL... WHAT IS MORE, HE DOES NOT SUFFER FROM THAT INSIDIOUS VIRUS OF GUILT, AND HE IS ABSOLUTELY IMMUNE TO SHAME...A TRUE WARRIOR...
WOZ 01

WATCH OUT...
...BLUEBERRY IS SMOKING! TOBACCO.
NO, THIS WON'T DO! I ABSOLUTELY CAN'T **CONDONE** THESE IDEAS!
HEY, **CHILL OUT!**
YOU NEED TO UNDERSTAND, ABOVE ALL, THAT BIN AND I ARE DESERT WARRIORS.
DESERT WARRIORS KNOW NEITHER SHAME, NOR GUILT, NOR FEAR... AND THIS WILL SURPRISE YOU, BUT NEITHER DO WE KNOW ANGER.
WE ARE THE SERPENT THAT BITES, WITHOUT HESITATION, ANY FLESH PENETRATING OUR TERRITORY.
WE ARE THE SCORPION THAT JABS ITS POISONOUS STINGER INTO ANY THREATENING FLESH.
I JUST CAN'T STAND IT.
MŒBIUS 01

IT'S LIKE OIL AND WATER DOWN THERE! THE AUTHOR IS LEAVING THE STAGE.

CROOOT!

THE MAJOR WILL END UP ALONE WITH THOSE TWO LUNATIC TERROR-ISTS!

HEY! DON'T GO!

THAT'S HIS THING! ANY CONFLICT AND HE'S GONE!

I DON'T WANT TO HEAR ANY MORE!

OR EVEN SEE--

MOEB 01

COME BACK! DO NOT LEAVE LIKE THIS!
LET HIM GO, BIN! HE'S JUST A PALEFACE. LIKE ALL THE REST, HE CAN'T LOOK CERTAIN TRUTHS IN THE FACE.
PFFT!
DRIII
DRIIII
DOODLE-OOOO
DOODLE-OOOO
"PFFT" WHAT?
REGARDING... TRUTHS!
I HAVE A FEW COMMENTS TO MAKE...
HELLO?
FIRST, I MUST SAY THAT A LACK OF GUILTY FEELING, IN MY OPINION, HASN'T ANY ADVANTAGES. GUILT PROMPTS REFLECTION. IT PROMOTES AN INCREASE IN OUR FACULTY OF JUDGMENT. IT EXPANDS CONSCIOUSNESS TO THE OUTER LIMITS OF PERCEPTION.
WALL STREET.
YES? IT'S DOWN?
MOEB 01

I CAN'T HELP BUT THINK ABOUT THE TAR'HAI SORCERER AND THE MENACE OF THE BAKALITE.

NO! SELL!

WHO ARE THEY?

AS FOR YOU, GERONIMO, YOUR LIFE FORCE IS SO VESTED IN SURVIVAL THAT IT'S TRANSFORMED YOU INTO A KILLING MACHINE.
HUH! YOU AND YOUR COLONIAL GETUP! HOW COULD YOU THINK OTHERWISE?
HEY!
YOU SEE ME AS AN IMPERIALIST, AS THE OVUM VIEWS THE SPERM CELL ARRIVING TO FERTILIZE IT.
WHAT DID YOU SAY? **WHAT DID YOU SAY?!**
NADINE WALDIC!
BUT...WAIT... STOP!
I SHALL KILL YOU! INFIDEL DOG!
COOL, BIN.
HEY, MIKE! A LITTLE HELP HERE?
PIF
PAF
MŒB 01

NO NEED! I FIGURE THE MAJOR'S GOT THIS.

YOU SHOULD BE ASHAMED, BEHAVING LIKE THIS IN A COMIC THAT ISN'T EVEN YOURS.
WHITE DEVIL! YOU CAN HUNT ME DOWN OR EVEN KILL ME-- ANOTHER WILL TAKE MY PLACE.

NOT NECESSARILY!
I EXPECT THE AUTHOR WILL BE RATHER MORE CIRCUMSPECT FROM NOW ON AND WILL BETTER ATTEND TO THE GENRE'S BOUNDARIES.
YOUR AUTHOR IS NOTHING BUT A PAPER DEVIL!

I RECOGNIZE ONLY ONE AUTHOR-- GOD... I MEAN, ALLAH!

AS TO THAT, BIN, I HAVE MORE TO SAY. LISTEN HERE!

YOU'RE PROBABLY NOT AWARE OF THIS, BUT I COME FROM THE FUTURE... FROM A TIME WHEN ALL RELIGIONS HAVE DIED OUT.

PERHAPS YOU WISHED TO DEFEND ISLAM...
...BUT ALL THE HISTORY BOOKS OF MY ERA POSIT SEPTEMBER 11 AS THE START OF YOUR RELIGION'S DEMISE.

ALLAH, ON THE OTHER HAND, IS STILL AROUND!
INFIDEL DOG!

I SHALL KILL YOU!
BIN! STOP.
THE AUTHOR WILL ALLOW YOU MANY THINGS, BUT HE WILL CERTAINLY NOT LET YOU KILL ME.
I STILL CANNOT PERMIT YOU TO SAY SUCH A THING... ISLAM MUST NOT CEASE... IT...IT IS UNTHINKABLE.
I SHOULD LIKE TO BELIEVE THAT.
BUT...WHAT **WILL** ABSOLUTELY DIE OUT, AND OF ITS OWN ACCORD, IS SHARIA LAW. YOU'LL NOT ELUDE DEMOCRACY OR SECULARISM... OR EVEN GUILT.
I SHALL KILL YOU WITH NO MORE REMORSE THAN I'D SPARE ANY IMPERIALIST CUR!
SEE? THEY'RE WORKIN' IT OUT.
YOU PALEFACES ARE ALL THE SAME.
YOU TWIST EVERYTHING AROUND WITH THOSE FORKED TONGUES OF YOURS.
SO... MAY WE JOIN THEM NOW?
I BELIEVE THE MOMENT HAS ARRIVED!
MOEB 01

19

WILL YOU COME WITH US?
NAH... BETTER NOT. ANYWAY, I GOT SOMETHIN' MORE IMPORTANT TO DO.

BEFORE YOU GO, TELL ME... DO YOU KNOW THOSE TWO FLYERS WHO JUST TURNED UP, ABOVE?

OH, HIM? THAT'S ARZAK! A FELLA FROM THE FUTURE. YOU'LL LIKE 'IM.

MM...AND THE OTHER?
NO IDEA! OKAY, SO... THIS HAS BEEN SWELL, BUT I GOTTA HEAD OUT FOR NEW ADVENTURES!

WATCH OUT FOR THAT DUDE WITH THE TURBAN. I DON'T TRUST HIM AN INCH.
I'LL BE CAREFUL. HE'S TOO MUCH LIKE ME TO BE TRUSTED.
YOU, TOO... WATCH OUT FOR YOURSELF.
MŒBIUS 01

20
AMZAK!
I AM GERONIMO.

ARZAK IS HERE. I WONDER WHO'S WITH HIM.
DO NOT ALLOW YOURSELF TO BE DISTRACTED. SIT DOWN AND HAVE A CUP OF SCENTED TEA. WE NEED TO WRAP UP THIS INTERESTING CONVERSATION.
THIS STORY'S CRAP. I DON'T EVEN KNOW WHERE TO GO.
DAMN IT!
MATTER O' FACT--I LIED! I DON'T HAVE **ANY** NEW ADVENTURE TO GET TO! NO DIALOGUE, NO SCRIPT. NADA!
...
I NEED TO GET MY HANDS ON THAT GUY GIR!
MŒBIUS 01

IN SEARCH O' MY OWN AUTHOR...DOWN TO THIS! JEAN-MICHAEL CHARLIER WOULDA NEVER **DARED...**

DAMN IT! AND IT COULD BE THAT MY BEIN' HERE ISN'T EVEN LEGAL!

BLOODY HELL. WHERE'S HE HIDIN'?

?

AN' WHAT THE HELL IS THIS THING?

MOEB 01

SOME KINDA FUTURISTIC PENCIL! IT'S GOTTA BE HIS! I'M ON THE RIGHT TRAIL.
PILOT
WHAT'RE THEY UP TO?
THEY BANDY WORDS. LET THEM FINISH.
USUALLY, THE MAJOR ISN'T SO TALKATIVE.
I APOLOGIZE FOR THREATENING YOU, BUT I AM UNDER SOME PRESSURE AT THE MOMENT.
AND I APOLOGIZE FOR FAILING IN MY DISCRETIONARY DUTY BY REVEALING ASPECTS OF THE FUTURE...

IT WAS IDIOTIC SINCE, AT HEART, ISLAM LEAVES ME RATHER INDIFFERENT...

NOW, THAT IS SHARIA!
NOT AT ALL!

I DO NOT REALLY BELIEVE IN ISLAM AS A POLITICAL SYSTEM...

...NOT LONG TERM, AT LEAST.
THAT'S GOOD TO HEAR!!!

WHO CAN KNOW THE WILL OF ALLAH?
NO ONE EXCEPT A PROPHET!
YOU, PERHAPS.

I BELIEVE BUT THIS: MY COLLEAGUES AND I HAVE DEDICATED OUR LIVES TO OUR PEOPLE'S FATE.

I KNOW MANY WHO DO THE SAME FOR THE FATE OF ALL HUMANITY...

HAHAHA!

?

WHAT'S SO FUNNY?

I FIND YOU QUITE POMPOUS FOR A MAN FROM THE FUTURE!

WHY MUST THE AUTHOR INFLICT THIS INCESSANT CONVERSATION ON US? IN MY DAY, HE DIDN'T BURDEN HIMSELF WITH WORDS!

STRAIGHT UP! BUT TIMES CHANGE. HEY...WHO'S YOUR BUDDY? **HE** HASN'T SAID A THING.

THAT'S ***MALVINA!*** THE COMMANDER OF THE CIGURI...

SHE'S ALSO THE MAJOR'S PARTNER.

OH, A WOMAN! AND A PRETTY ***HOT*** ONE, BESIDES! BUT HOW IS IT SHE LOVES A MAN WITH SUCH A TINY... MUSTACHE?

PLEASE! STOP PLAYING THE INDIAN SIDEKICK!

26

HAVE YOU NEVER READ ANY MUSLIM OR BUDDHIST SCIENCE FICTION? YOU CATEGORICALLY ALIGN YOURSELF WITH THE DESTINY OF **ALL** HUMANITY! WHICH IS THE GREAT LIE OF THE WEST!

WHO SAYS IT'S A LIE? AND I MUST POINT OUT THAT YOU HAPPEN TO BE **IN** A SCIENCE FICTION STORY AT THIS VERY MOMENT.

I AM NEITHER IN LITERATURE NOR IN SHOWBIZ...**MY** WORK IS INSCRIBED IN REALITY. I HAVE CREATED A MYTHOLOGY THAT HAS NOT ONLY CHANGED THE WORLD BUT THAT WILL BE FOREVER ENGRAVED IN COLLECTIVE MEMORY.

I WORK FOR HUMANITY, THOUGH I DO NOT IDENTIFY WITH IT...YOU WHO KNOW THE FUTURE, I DARE YOU TO TELL ME OTHERWISE...
I'D BE WARY OF THAT, BIN.
MŒBIUS 01

FOR YEARS, THE COLLAPSE OF THE TOWERS WAS JUST AS NOTORIOUS AS THE PARTING OF THE RED SEA...
...OR THE MASSACRE OF THE INNOCENTS...
NOT BAD.
BUT ALL THOSE OLD MYTHS WERE EVENTUALLY FORGOTTEN.
GOOD!
AS TO THE FATE OF YOUR PEOPLE...THEY FELL INTO THE PLANETARY MELTING POT ONCE EARTH WAS ADMITTED INTO COSMOCIVILIZATION.
COSMO-CIVILIZATION.
THIS IS LONG!
TOO LONG!
WELL, YES! EXTRA-TERRESTRIALS AND ALL THAT...
LOOK! SPEAKING OF ETs, HERE COMES ONE NOW!
MŒBIUS 01

DO MAKE YOURSELVES COMFY. THERE'S TEA FOR EVERYONE.
YOU WERE A BIT LONG-WINDED.
HELLO!
WE WERE GETTING IMPATIENT.
THAT FELLOW IS AN EXTRATERRESTRIAL? HE DOES NOT SEEM TO BE...TO ME, HE IS BUT ANOTHER INFIDEL DOG.
HELLO, MALVINA.
HELLO, MAJOR.
WHAT'S UP, BIN? WHY THE LONG FACE?
OHHH, THE MAJOR AND HIS FUTURE ARE A DRAG...BUT THAT WILL NOT STOP ME IN MY CRUSADE.
YOUR **CRUSADE**?
MY JIHAD! SAME DIFF.

WHERE'S MIKE? HE WAS WITH YOU EARLIER, WASN'T HE?
HE LEFT! IN SEARCH OF THE AUTHOR, I'D GUESS.
GOOD IDEA! WITHOUT **HIM,** THIS PLACE LOOKS LIKE A **REAL** DESERT.
DRIII DRIII DOODLE-OOOO

HELLO ?
HELLO, OMAR? YES! IT'S ME, BIN.
WHAT? AMERICAN ZIONISTS BOMBED THE COUNTRY? THOSE TERRORISTS! GET **ACCOUNTING** ON THE LINE!
HURRY! CIAO!
GOOD GRIEF! CELLPHONES SHOULD BE TURNED OFF DURING THE NARRATIVE.

MIKE IS STRONG, BUT IF MOEB **REALLY** WANTS TO HIDE, MIKE WILL NEVER FIND HIM.
SO, WE'RE STUCK HERE FOR A WHILE...

DAMN IT! I'VE BEEN GOIN' IN CIRCLES FOR HOURS...I MEAN, WANDERIN' AROUND THIS ROCKY MAZE...

?
THERE...A MEXICAN!
HOWDY, STRANGER! HAVE YOU MAYBE SEEN A MAN IN THESE PARTS, IN HIS SIXTIES, WEARIN' GLASSES?
HELLO.
COULD BE...
MŒB01

I'LL ANSWER YOUR QUESTION IF YOU ANSWER MINE. HAVE YOU SEEN A VERY BEAUTIFUL, ALMOST NAKED BLONDE WOMAN GOING IN CIR--**UH,** WANDERING AR--**UH,** WHO SEEMS A LITTLE LOST IN THIS DESERT?

HMM...

A VERY BEAUTIFUL WOMAN, BLONDE, ALMOST NAKED, WHO... UH...LET'S SEE.

HER NAME IS ATANA...

OHHH! HER! ATANA!!! YEP... I SAW HER!

ARE YOU SURE? WHERE? WHERE ***IS*** SHE?

WELL...OVER THAT WAY! STRAIGHT AHEAD, THEN TAKE A LEFT... AN' ANOTHER LEFT... THEN RIGHT FOR ABOUT HALF A MILE. SHE WAS THERE JUST A WHILE AGO... UH...TOTALLY NAKED!

32
HEY! AND MY QUESTION! DID YOU FORGET?
I DIDN'T FORGET!

SO...? WAIT!
THAT GUY'S SURE GOT A PAIR. WHAT AN ASS!
MŒBIUS

WELL, I DIDN'T SEE HIS ATANA WOMAN ANYWAY...
...AND NO MATTER WHICH ROAD I TAKE, IF THE AUTHOR **WANTS** TO SEE ME, HE'LL BE WAITIN' FOR ME AT THE END.
OKAY! I'LL HEAD RIGHT!
HELLO? ACCOUNTING? PUT ME THROUGH TO ACCOUNTING!
ALI?
MOEBIUS

GIVE ME MAHFOUZ!
HELLO? ALI? WHERE ARE THE MICROFOST SHARES? WHAT? HE WISHES TO TALK TO ME?
HELLO? BILL BRIDGE? YES, IT IS ME, BIN. HOW ARE YOU?
NO.
YUP.

I...I SHALL BE AVENGED! GODLESS DOG! EATER OF PIGS!

I WILL SEND MY KILLERS YOUR WAY... MY CUTTHROATS...THUGS WITHOUT PITY!
MY SUICIDE BOMBERS.
POISONED MAIL.
WHAT ?

YOU DO NOT GIVE A DAMN? CLEARLY, YOU DO NOT KNOW TO WHOM YOU SPEAK, YOU LITTLE WHITE ASSHOLE!

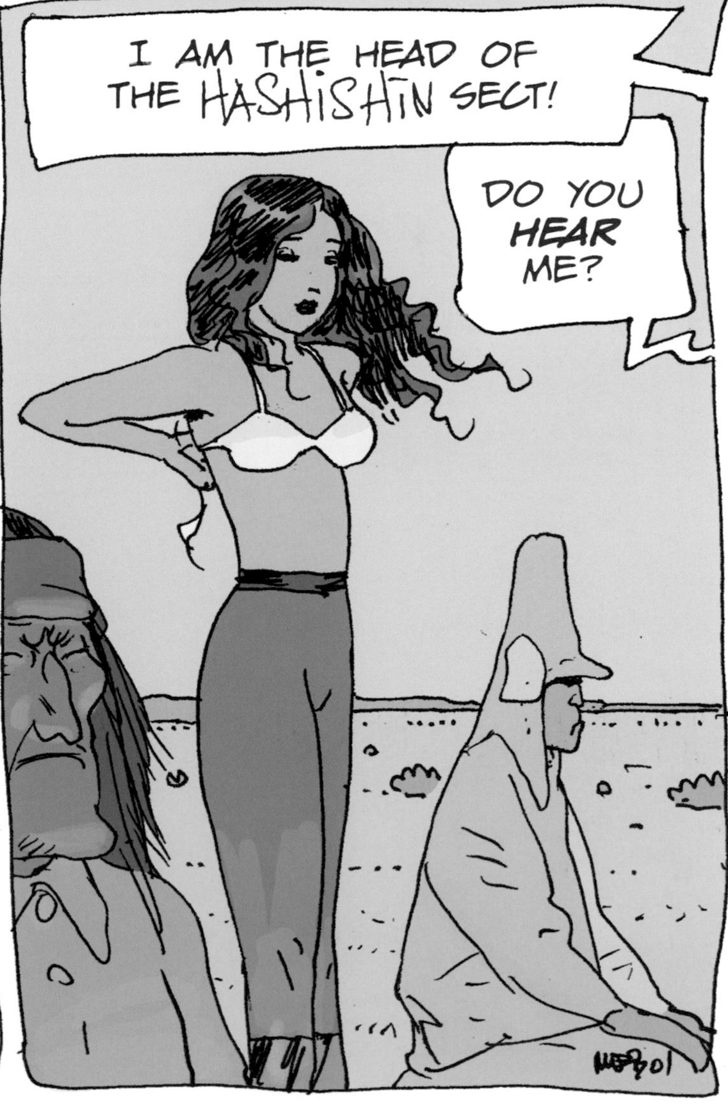
I AM THE HEAD OF THE HASHISHIN SECT!
DO YOU **HEAR** ME?

SHIT! I SPEAK IN A VACUUM! THE BATTERY IS DEAD!

WESTERN TECHNOLOGY PIECE OF SHIT!
CRASH

AND THAT MICROFOST MOTHERFUCKER WHO TOSSED MY EQUITY SHARES IN THE SHITTER! I AM RUINED! COMPLETELY CLEANED OUT!!!

DON'T FRET, MY HAIRY ONE! WE HAVE A SAYING... "UNLUCKY AT CARDS, LUCKY IN LOVE."
?!!
BUT! WHAT? WAIT! OH...

...NOOOO!
GET BACK! DO NOT COME NEAR ME! DO NOT TOUCH ME!
WHAT ARE YOU AFRAID OF? I COME TO YOU UNARMED!

BUT I CAN FULFILL ALL YOUR DESIRES.
ALLAH! DELIVER ME FROM EVIL! DELIVER ME!
YOU ARE EVIL!

YOUR WISH WILL BE GRANTED IMMEDI-ATELY!

LOOK AT ME.

LET ME HEAL YOU, BIN! YOU'RE ILL! VERY ILL!
YOU ARE ONE OF THE DJINN! A DEMON STRAIGHT OUT OF THE LEGIONS OF HELL! YOU ARE... A WOMAN!

IT'S HIM ALL RIGHT.

BUT... WHAT THE HELL'S HE UP TO?

oooOOOAoooHOA!

DAMN! HE'S GONE CRAZY!
OOOATUAHH!

oooOOoooUUU!
YAAAR!

OUCH.

THERE YOU GO! YOU'RE AFRAID OF WOMEN... AND THAT IS WHAT MAKES ALL OF YOU UNHEALTHY.
YOU DO NOT FRIGHTEN ME! I HATE YOU TOO MUCH.
SOME TEA?
GLADLY!

YOU KNOW THE THREE BASES OF HATRED-- DECEPTION, FRUSTRATION, AND HUMILIATION! I'LL HEAL YOU WITH LOVE AND HELP YOU UNDERSTAND YOUR OWN SOUL.
DEMON!

NO!
OH! NO.

WHAT DID YOU DO?
FROM NOW ON...
...YOUR SOUL IS NOT AN ISLAND.

DEMON!
DEMON FROM HELL! WHY HAVE YOU DONE THIS?
WHY?
TO TEACH YOU, BINNY!
GASP!
WHAT'S WRONG? IS HE DEAD?
NO! HE JUST FAINTED.
GOOD GRIEF! WHAT DID YOU DO TO THE POOR MAN?
YOU KNOW PERFECTLY WELL...I SIMPLY FOLLOWED THE PATH OF HIS FEAR AND ANGER...
...TO HIS HIDDEN DESIRE.
MOEB 01

BUT...
MY STARS, MALVINA! THAT'S JUST DREADFUL! AND OBSCENE!
OH, NO... NO...

IT'S ACTUALLY RATHER MONSTROUS, YOU MUST ADMIT! AND I KNOW MY MONSTERS, INSIDE AND OUT...
OH, DON'T EXAGGERATE, YOU TWO!
EGAD!

BIG G...I'M SURE ***YOU*** UNDERSTAND WHAT I DID...

YOU BET! YOU USED YOUR SEXUAL SORCERY POWER TO CURE HIM! YOU'VE MADE HIM A DIFFERENT MAN!

NOT BAD!

HEH HEH!

MŒBIUS 01

LISTEN! SEXUAL SIBYLS AREN'T SOME KIND OF SUPER-WHORES HATCHED IN THE SICK MIND OF AN OBSESSED PERVERT-- SEXUAL SIBYLS ARE MASTERS IN THEIR FIELD!

EXACTLY.

MASTERS!

AND IT WAS A DELEGATION OF WOMEN FROM KABUL WHO ENTRUSTED ME WITH THIS SPECIAL JIHAD.
HOLY COW!

HOLY SHIT! I CAN'T DO THIS ANYMORE.

MY BACK! YOWCH!
OW.
OW.
OKAY! I'LL TRY AGAIN TOMORROW! IT'LL COME BACK.
THIS IS MY VERY OWN COMIC. I MUSTN'T FORGET.
EVER!
BLOODY HELL.
MOE301

POOR OLD GUY'S GONE TOTALLY SENILE!
FOR A MINUTE THERE, HE REALLY SEEMED TO THINK HE WAS A GODDAMN BIRD!
NOW WHAT SHOULD I DO?
SINCE I STILL DON'T HAVE A SCRIPT.
I'M GONNA HAVE TO DO SOMETHIN' ALL ON MY OWN...
MOEB 01

LUCKILY I STILL HAVE MY MIND...MY MEMORIES!

I CAN'T FLY ANYMORE...
...BUT I CAN REMEMBER.
LET'S GO...

...TO WORK..

LIKE A DREAM!

GOOD GRIEF! THIS PLACE IS GIGANTIC.
ILLUSTRATIONS 1957 · 1958
I'D BETTER NOT GET LOST.
ANYWAY... NOBODY WILL RECOGNIZE ME THANKS TO THIS COSTUME, WHICH I PILFERED FROM THE PROP ROOM...
NOBODY!
EVERY ONE O' THESE DOORS MUST LEAD TO HIS ARCHIVES...

ALL THOSE YEARS OF WORK...GLUED TO THE DRAWING BOARD.
PUBS
FILMS
AND SO IT GOES...
WESTERNS
THERE! THERE!
SF
WEST
OH-HO!

INCREDIBLE! ALL THE ORIGINAL ART BOARDS FROM CHIHUAHUA PEARL, THE LOST DUTCHMAN'S MINE, AND MORE!
GONE FOREVER.
THOUGHT THEY WERE LOST.

STRANGE!
HE'S GONNA OWE ME SOME EXPLA- NATIONS!
I REALLY LIKE THIS ONE.
MŒBIUS 01

WHAT'S ALL THIS ABOUT A DELEGATION OF WOMEN FROM KABUL?

WE HAVE TO DO SOME-THING! WE CAN'T LEAVE HIM LIKE THIS.

IT'S A GIRL THING. CHILL.

A CONVOCATION OF SEXUAL SIBYLS WAS HELD ON CALLISTO, IN THE CYGNUS CONSTELLATION.

PLEASE! STOP SHAKING. I CAN'T SEE YOU CLEARLY!

I DON'T KNOW WHAT'S HAPPENING... IT'S THE AUTHOR WHO...WHO...

JOHN!
STOP.

IT'S STRONGER THAN I AM.

JOHN!

OKAY, NOW?
IT WASN'T ME, I SWEAR.
OKAY.
I KNOW. IT'S MOEB. HE'S CAPABLE OF ANY-THING.

THAT WOMAN IS A DEMON. WHAT SHE HAS DARED DO TO ME IS CRIMINAL!
THE REAL CULPRIT IS THIS MOEBIUS... A SPIRIT WHO LIVES IN THE DREAM WORLD.
HIM AGAIN? MAY HE BE DAMNED!

I SHALL NOT TAKE ONE MORE STEP. I HAVE HAD ENOUGH!
ME, TOO.
AND YOU KNOW...

...I AM NOT A BEING MADE OF PAPER TO WHOM ONE CAN DO ANYTHING.
SAME HERE. I'M A REAL HUMAN, LIKE YOU.
HMM...HOWEVER...

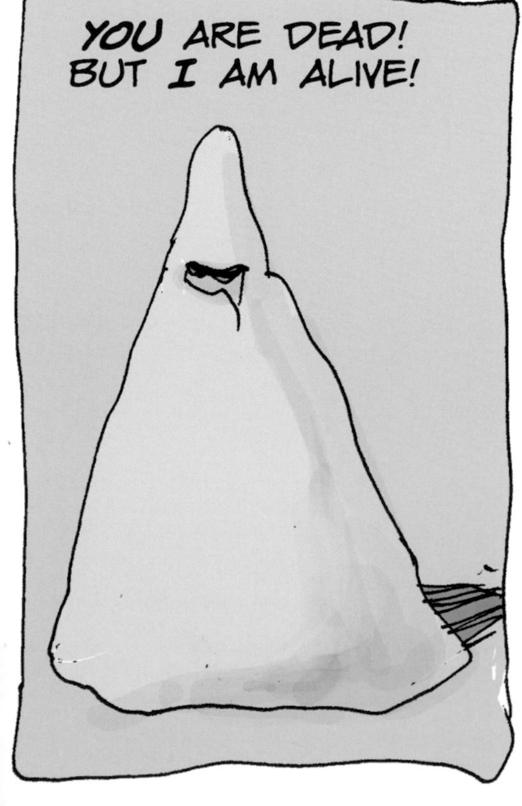
YOU ARE DEAD! BUT I AM ALIVE!

WHAT? I'M DEAD?! ME? GERONIMO?!

DEAD!
YUP! DEAD!

THIS CONVOCATION OF SIBYLS WAS IMPORTANT... WOMEN OF ALL RACES, FROM ALL OVER THE GALAXY... FREE WOMEN, BRIMMING WITH LOVE AND PRIDE, MOST OF THEM GIFTED WITH GREAT POWER. THE KABUL DELEGATION SOUGHT ME OUT ONCE WORD GOT AROUND THAT I WAS TO COME HERE AND MEET WITH BIN LADEN...
I HAD NO IDEA THAT OUR "FRIEND" WAS SO WELL KNOWN IN THE FAR-OFF FUTURE.

HE'S BECOME THE SYMBOL OF FEMALE OPPRESSION, JUST AS HITLER REPRESENTS JEWISH PERSECUTION.
AND...WHAT ABOUT THE SEPTEMBER 11 ATTACKS?

OH...NO... THAT ALL ENDED UP BEING FORGOT-TEN.
WHEREAS FEMALE MARTYRDOM... HAS NOT.

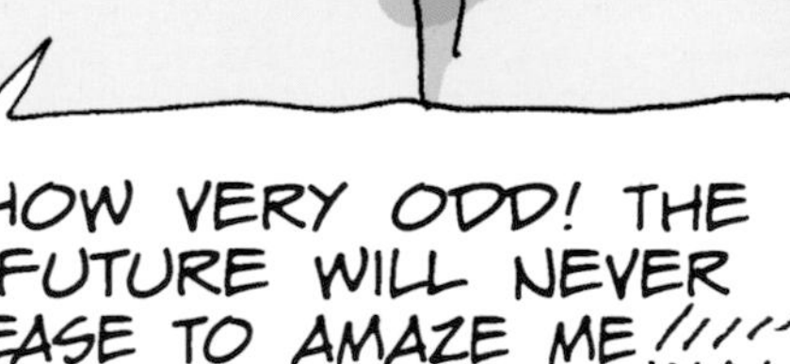
HOW VERY ODD! THE FUTURE WILL NEVER CEASE TO AMAZE ME!!!!!
MOEBIUS 01

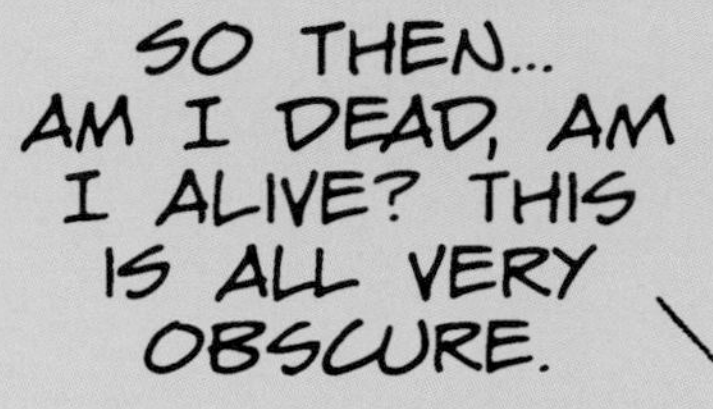
SO THEN... AM I DEAD, AM I ALIVE? THIS IS ALL VERY OBSCURE.
JUST LIKE EVERYTHING THESE INFIDEL DOGS DO...THEY ARE DUPLICITOUS, SUSPICIOUS, CAPRICIOUS...
THEIR TONGUES ARE FORKED.
EVEN THEIR SEXUALITY HAS BECOME UNDIFFERENTIATED... OR INDIFFERENT.

THEY SPEAK OF THE FUTURE.
THE ONLY FUTURE... IS DEATH.
THEY RUN FROM SUFFERING.
SUFFERING IS THE MOTHER OF ALL HOPE.

CREATING ADVERSITY IS THE SINGLE FREEDOM THAT REMAINS...
...BUT...

...WHAT THAT SHE-DEVIL DID TO ME IS NOT ADVERSITY... IT IS DEFILEMENT!
DEFILE-MENT ?!

YOU MEAN THAT YOUR TRANSFORMATION TO A FEMALE HAS **DEFILED** YOU?
YES.
BUT...BECOMING FEMALE DOESN'T MAKE YOU A **WOMAN!**
YOU ARE RIGHT! IN MY MIND, I AM STILL A **MAN!**
YEAH, HEY! IT'S ALL IN THE MIND!
IN MY MIND I KNOW THAT I AM REAL, ALIVE, AND A MAN...BUT NOT HERE... HERE, I AM MADE OF PAPER. I AM NO MORE THAN THE **PUPPET** OF A **COMIC BOOK** CREATOR.
AND YET...I KNOW THAT, AT HEART, HE FEARS ME... I FRIGHTEN HIM... HE IS AFRAID OF ME... AFRAID OF **US**.
IT'S TRUE!
HA HA!

HA HA HA!
HA HA HA!

HA HAHA!
HAHAHAHA!

MŒB 01

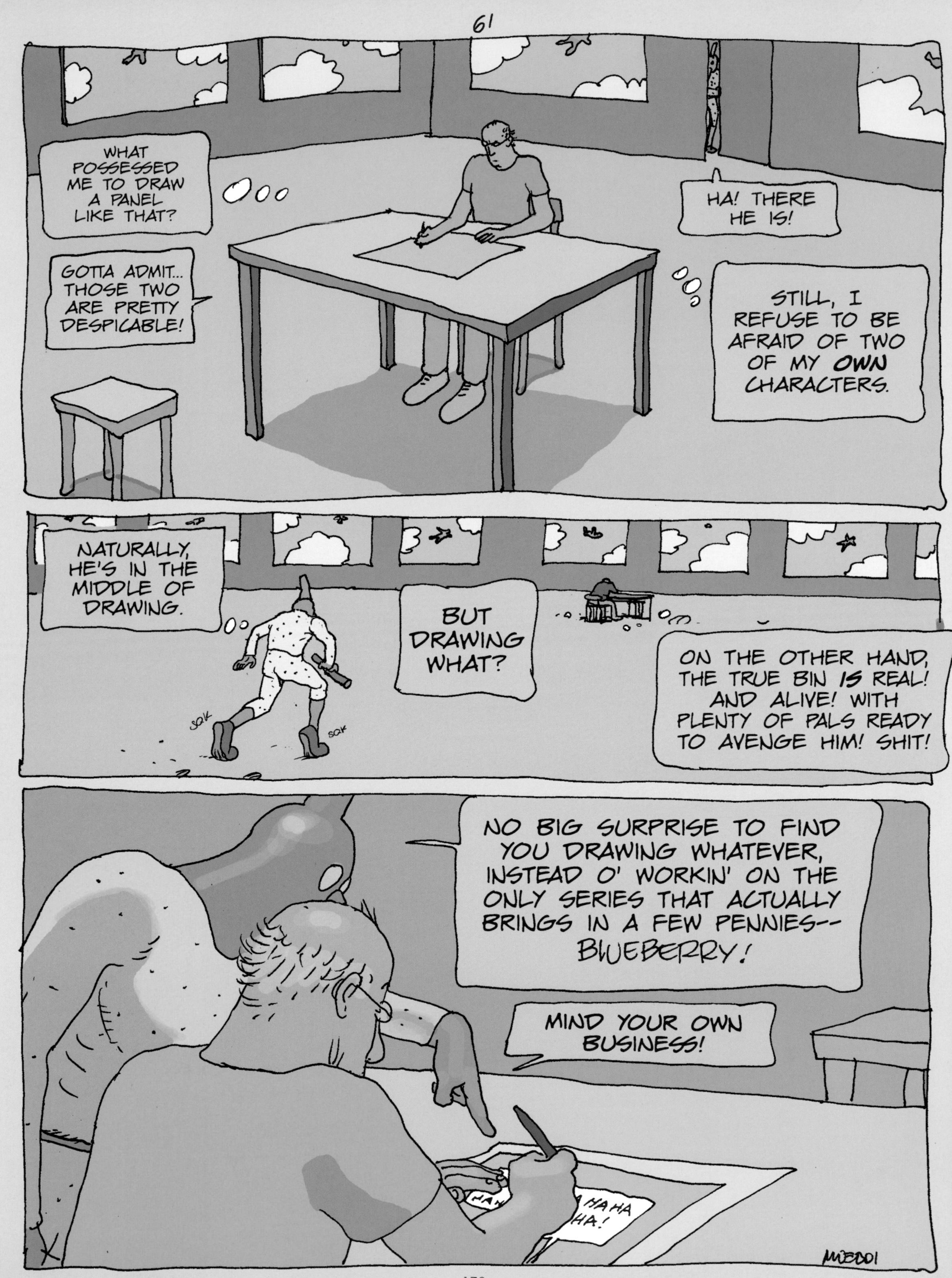
WHAT POSSESSED ME TO DRAW A PANEL LIKE THAT?
HA! THERE HE IS!
GOTTA ADMIT... THOSE TWO ARE PRETTY DESPICABLE!
STILL, I REFUSE TO BE AFRAID OF TWO OF MY OWN CHARACTERS.
NATURALLY, HE'S IN THE MIDDLE OF DRAWING.
BUT DRAWING WHAT?
SQK
SQK
ON THE OTHER HAND, THE TRUE BIN IS REAL! AND ALIVE! WITH PLENTY OF PALS READY TO AVENGE HIM! SHIT!
NO BIG SURPRISE TO FIND YOU DRAWING WHATEVER, INSTEAD O' WORKIN' ON THE ONLY SERIES THAT ACTUALLY BRINGS IN A FEW PENNIES-- BLUEBERRY!
MIND YOUR OWN BUSINESS!
HAHA
HA!
MŒBIUS

KLOTZ CAME UP WITH A BASIC OUTLINE FOR YOU THAT'S MORE THAN FINE, BUT YOU KEEP ON WITH ALL THIS STUFF THAT NO ONE CARES ABOUT, YOU PAIN IN THE ASS.
NO ONE?
NO ONE!

AND NOW YOU'RE EVEN BAD-MOUTHIN' REAL PEOPLE! HAVE YOU THOUGHT ABOUT THE CONSE-QUENCES?

SURE I REALIZE ALL THAT! BUT...IT'S STRONGER THAN I AM! THE STORY'S GOTTEN AWAY FROM ME!

GOOD GOD, YOU'RE TOTALLY IRRESPONSIBLE! BLUEBERRY IS WHAT YOU HAVE TO DRAW! GET IT?
HRG!

BAF
OKAY, THAT'S ENOUGH!

HEY! YOU... YOU BROKE MY SCHNOZ!
UH... SORRY.

I DON'T KNOW WHO YOU ARE, MISTER, BUT PLEASE JUST LET ME WORK IN PEACE!
GET IT?
MŒBIUS 01

YOU DON'T RECOGNIZE ME?
I DON'T GIVE A DAMN! I DON'T EVEN WANT TO KNOW! I'M AT HOME HERE. IN MY COMIC! IN MY DESERT!
MY DESERT "B."
I BET YOU DON'T EVEN HAVE A CLUE WHAT THAT "B" STANDS FOR! WELL, IT'S "B" AS IN "BIS"... IT'S EARTH-TWO...WHERE MY DOUBLE IS ALL-POWERFUL.
SO, YOU'RE HEAD OF STATE-TWO.
RIGHT! I'M THE MASTER COMMANDER HERE! I'M GOD!
OR, RATHER, GOED!
MŒB01

GOED? REALLY, TRULY GOED?
BUT IF YOU ARE MASTER COMMANDER, HOW'S THIS STORY GETTIN' AWAY FROM YOU?
BECAUSE OF SOMETHING STRONGER THAN YOU! THOSE ARE YOUR WORDS!
HM!
THAT, MY LITTLE MAN, IS THE MYSTERY OF ART!
THE MYSTERY OF ART!
NO QUESTION! IT IS STRONG!
THE MYSTERY OF ART!
I GAVE IT TO BIN. HE WANTED TO HIDE HIS NEW FEMALE ANATOMY.
POOR GUY! HE WAS DYING OF SHAME! ON THE OTHER HAND, HE DIDN'T FEEL GUILTY.
ARZAK, DO JOIN US! THERE'S STILL SOME TEA LEFT. BUT... WHERE'S YOUR CAPE? THAT FINE HEROIC FANTASY CAPE?
IT NEEDS TO STEEP A WHILE!
MOEB 01

WE WERE JUST TALKING ABOUT KABUL IN THE FUTURE...A FANTASTIC MEGALOPOLIS...A GORGEOUS GARDEN WHERE MEN AND WOMEN FREELY LOVE--AND LEAVE--EACH OTHER.
IT'S TRUE! ONLY PEACE AND PLENTY ALLOW FOR SUCH A CRUEL, YET DELICIOUS GAME.
WHY DO YOU MAKE YOUR WOMEN SUFFER?
BECAUSE WE ARE SO WRETCHED THAT WE WISH TO DISAPPEAR.
IT IS IN THIS WAY THAT POPULATIONS SOMETIMES TRY TO SELF-DESTRUCT... BY PERSECUTING THOSE WHO GIVE LIFE.*
*"THE ONLY SUCCESSFUL SUICIDES ARE FAILED SUICIDES." –C. BOBIN
MOEBIUS 01

YOU KNOW, AT THE MOMENT I DARED TO DEFY THE UNITED STATES, THAT COUNTRY WAS THE RICHEST AND MOST POWERFUL ON THIS PLANET, WHILE THE POOREST WERE THE AFGHANS...ONLY ONE NATION WAS RICHER THAN THE U.S.: **MY** NATION, WE WHO GUARD THE SACRED LAND.*

*THE REAL DEAL.

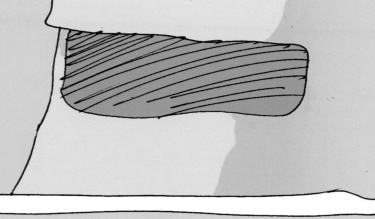

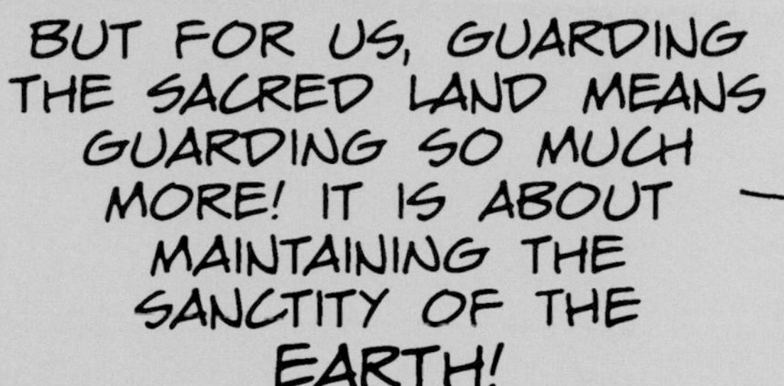

BUT FOR US, GUARDING THE SACRED LAND MEANS GUARDING SO MUCH MORE! IT IS ABOUT MAINTAINING THE SANCTITY OF THE EARTH!

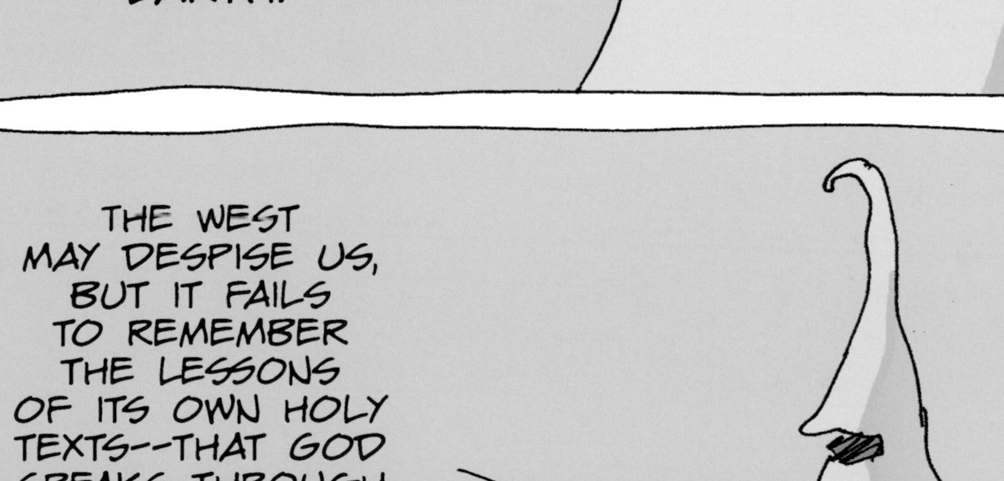

THE WEST MAY DESPISE US, BUT IT FAILS TO REMEMBER THE LESSONS OF ITS OWN HOLY TEXTS--THAT GOD SPEAKS THROUGH THE MOUTHS OF THE MOST HUMBLE... THE HUMILIATED... THE REJECTED...
MŒB 01

WHAT'S THAT? THE FIRST PAGE OF THE "OK CORRAL" STORY...?
NOT AT ALL!

IT'S ONE OF MY DAUGHTER'S DRAWINGS. NAUSICAÄ DRAWS RIDICULOUSLY WELL, DOESN'T SHE? HER ARZAK IS GREAT!
MOEB 01

ARZAK IS "GREAT"...? HA HA! DON'T MAKE ME LAUGH! HAVEN'T YOU SEEN THE SALES FIGURES?
THAT'S ENOUGH!

ARZAK REPRESENTS THE OTHERWORLDLY PERSPECTIVE! ABSOLUTELY INDISPENSABLE FOR UNDERSTANDING HUMAN BEHAVIOR!
PFFFT!

AND YOU, ARZAK... AS AN OUTWORLDER, WHAT DO YOU THINK OF ALL THIS?
OOH LA LA! THAT'S NOT EASY... SINCE OUR MORAL CHARTER DICTATES A DRACONIAN POLICY OF DIFFIDENCE.
GO ON! WE'RE IN AN **AMORAL** COMIC BOOK HERE!

BEFORE ALL ELSE, I'D LIKE TO POINT OUT TWO FAIRLY COMMON MISTAKES DURING THE PERIOD IN WHICH THESE EVENTS UNFOLD...
MISTAKES?
ONLY TWO?

YES, TWO MAJOR ERRORS IN MAN'S SELF-CONCEPT, IN THAT DISTANT TIME.

FIRST, THE BELIEF THAT MAN IS UNIQUE IN ALL OF CREATION...IT'S A SEMANTIC ERROR, TOO, LINKING ***MAN, HUMAN,*** AND ***HUMANITY.***

OF COURSE...

...AS A BIOLOGICAL PHENOMENON, MAN IS AS SINGULAR AS THE EARTH, BUT THIS ***IDEA*** OF HUMANITY, OR HUMAN, BELONGS TO THE ENTIRE UNIVERSE, IN ALL ITS ***VERY*** DIVERSE FORMS.

AND YET...***YOU*** HAVE A HUMAN APPEARANCE.

THAT'S AN UNDERSTANDING BETWEEN THE AUTHOR AND MYSELF. I ASSUME THIS LOOK OUT OF COMMERCIAL NECESSITY. MY REAL FORM, IN FACT, IS VERY DIFFERENT FROM WHAT YOU SEE HERE!

GO ON, THEN! SHOW US THE REAL THING!
BIG DEAL! WE DON'T GIVE A GODDAMN ABOUT THE READER! NOT HERE!
ALL RIGHT... BUT I WARN YOU, THERE'S A RISK OF SHOCKING SENSITIVE READERS!
TROiiiik!
VOOOZ...
OKAY, OKAY! WE'VE SEEN IT!

SO? WHAT DO YOU THINK?
THAT REMINDED ME OF MEN IN BLACK! BUT...YEAH! I LIKE YOU THIS WAY! STAY JUST AS YOU ARE NOW!
IT'S BETTER.
I DO UNDERSTAND WHAT YOU MEAN. NO MATTER ONE'S SHAPE OR COLOR, CONSCIENCE DETERMINES ONE'S MEMBERSHIP IN HUMANITY!

THIS IS THE SHOCK THAT AWAITS YOUR RACE...IS GOD THE FATHER OF THE EARTH OR OF THE UNIVERSE? AS FOR MYSELF...
...ALL BEINGS ARE MY BROTHERS AND SISTERS. I AM AS READY AS THEY TO LOVE OR HATE THEM, DEPENDING ON CIRCUMSTANCE AND MY OWN SENSIBILITY.

THAT SAID, THIS IS MY OPINION ONLY! I DON'T PROFESS TO REPRESENT THE MILLIONS OF BILLIONS OF BEINGS POPULATING THE GALAXY.

WHFF! WHAT THE HELL IS HE TALKING ABOUT? AND ANYWAY, WHAT DOES THAT OTHER ONE HAVE TO SAY?
MŒB301

I HEAR ALL YOUR ARGUMENTS !!!
BUT THEY RING FALSE IN MY WARRIOR'S HEART. YOU'VE LET YOURSELF BE MANIPULATED BY UNSCRUPULOUS GEOPOLITICAL POWER SYSTEMS. FOR THEM, HUMAN LIFE MEANS NOTHING, EVEN THE LIVES OF THEIR OWN PEOPLE. THIS POWER PLAY FOR YOUR MORAL SENSIBILITY FEEDS OFF YOUR PAIN AND CHILDISH ANGER.
NOT BAD FOR A SO-CALLED **SAVAGE,** HEY?!
BUT WAIT! THAT'S NOT ALL!
MOEB 01

OOH LA LA!

I'VE HAD ENOUGH!

NO! LET HIM SPEAK!

GERONIMO AND BIN ARE CONNECTED... THEY'RE DEALIN' WITH THE SAME ADVERSARY.

THAT'S A STRANGE OBSERVATION.

BUT... THERE'S AN ELEMENT OF TRUTH TO IT.

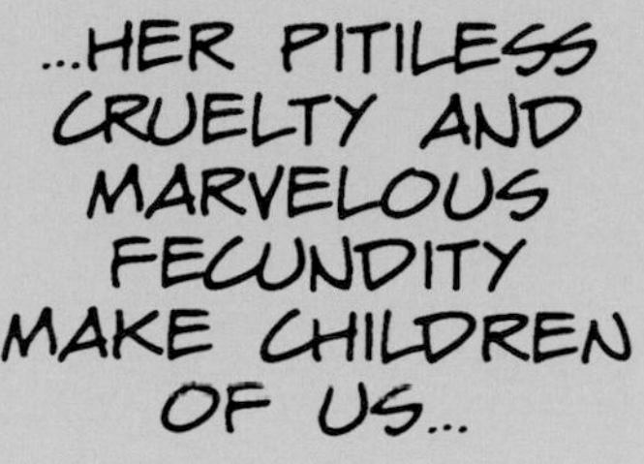

...HER PITILESS CRUELTY AND MARVELOUS FECUNDITY MAKE CHILDREN OF US...
...SPLIT BETWEEN DESTRUCTIVE HATRED AND SACRED LOVE... IN SOME WAYS, CONSCIENCE IS A KIND OF MADNESS, WHICH... IN A MOMENTARY FLASH...

...CONFERS THE ILLUSION OF DIVINE DESTINY ON THE CHAOS OF LIFE.
YOU ARE DEAD, AND I AM ALIVE! I SHALL LEAVE THIS WORLD OF PAPER AND RESUME MY FIGHT.
SURE! I'VE CROAKED...SO SCRAM! GO BACK TO THE REAL WORLD AND SLIT SOME PALEFACE THROAT!
INSH ALLAH.

WHATEVER YOUR MOTIVES... YOUR MADNESS HAS MADE YOU THE INSTRUMENT OF DIVINE DESTINY.
MOEB 01

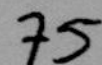

I CAN'T STAND IT ANYMORE! I QUIT! IT'S...IT'S TOO HARD!

I KNEW IT. YOU WANT TO GET BACK TO BASICS...

BLUEB!...

BLUE-BERRY BRINGS IN THE LOOT!

LEAVE ME THE HELL ALONE!

WAIT!

RAPHAEL

RAPHAEL

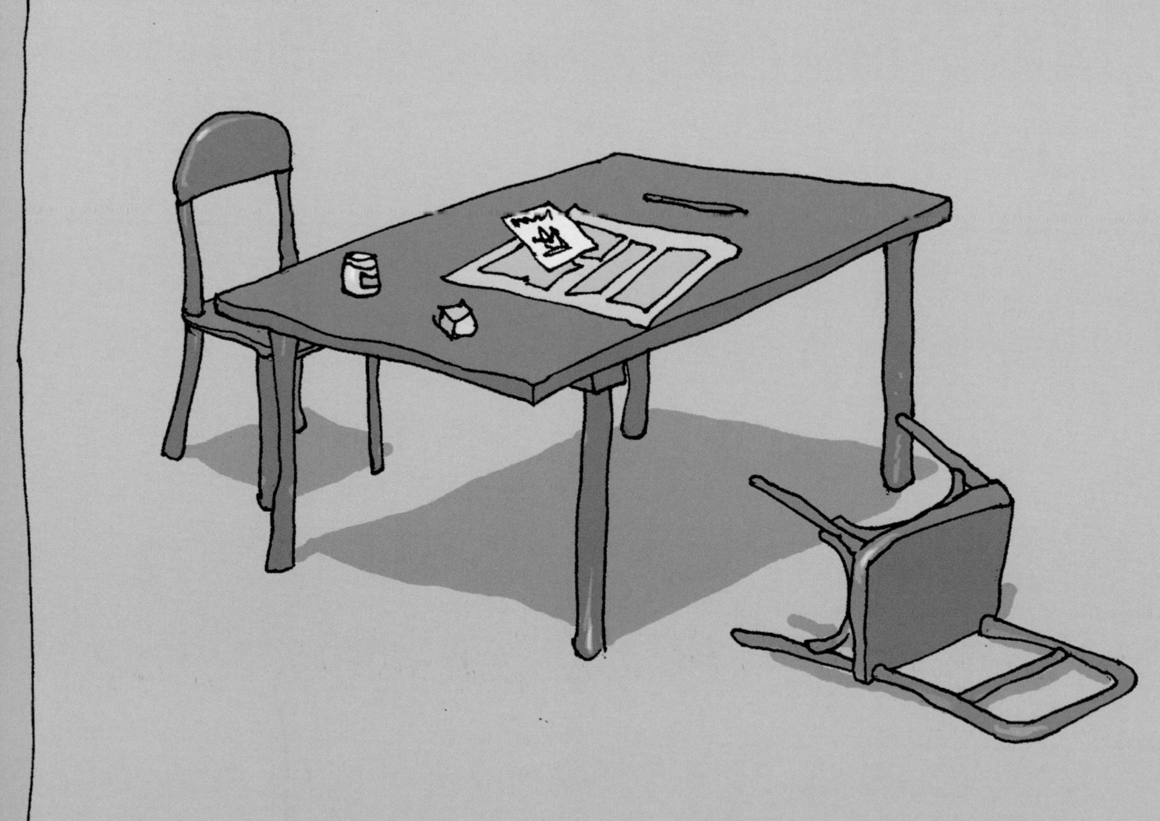

I SAID--
WAIT!
WHAT NOW?
IT'S THIS PAGE! THERE'S SOMETHIN' WEIRD ABOUT-- 
WHERE DID YOU FIND THAT *BLUEBERRY* ART?
MOEB 91

DOESN'T MATTER! WHAT'S GOT ME PUZZLED IS THAT IT'S NOT FROM ANY OF THE GRAPHIC NOVELS. THIS PAGE IS PART OF A STORY THAT WAS NEVER PUBLISHED...
TRUE.
BUT... THAT'S IMPOSSIBLE! J-M CHARLIER WOULDN'T HAVE AGREED TO THAT!
HE CERTAINLY WAS AWARE OF IT... LOOK! **HE** WROTE THE SCRIPT!
GASP!..
BUT...HOW COME **I** DON'T KNOW ABOUT THIS?
YOU? WHY?
UH...NO REASON. FORGET IT!
MŒBIUS 01

WHAT DO YOU THINK?
OH, NO... THIS IS TOO MUCH! I FEEL **SICK!**

THE ARTIST IS FREE TO WEAVE HIS WORLD AS HE SEES FIT. NO ONE KNOWS ABOUT THIS SECRET CHAPTER.
BUT...THE READERS!

THE FANS...THE EDITOR... THE PUBLISHER?
FUCK ALL OF THEM! LOOK-- I WANT TO SHOW YOU SOMETHING!
WHAT NOW?
CHECK IT OUT!

Y YAAAAOOOOOOO
MŒBIUS 01

THIS GUY'S TOTALLY NUTS!
HE **MUST** HAVE SMASHED INTO THE GROUND!
?
BLOODY HELL!

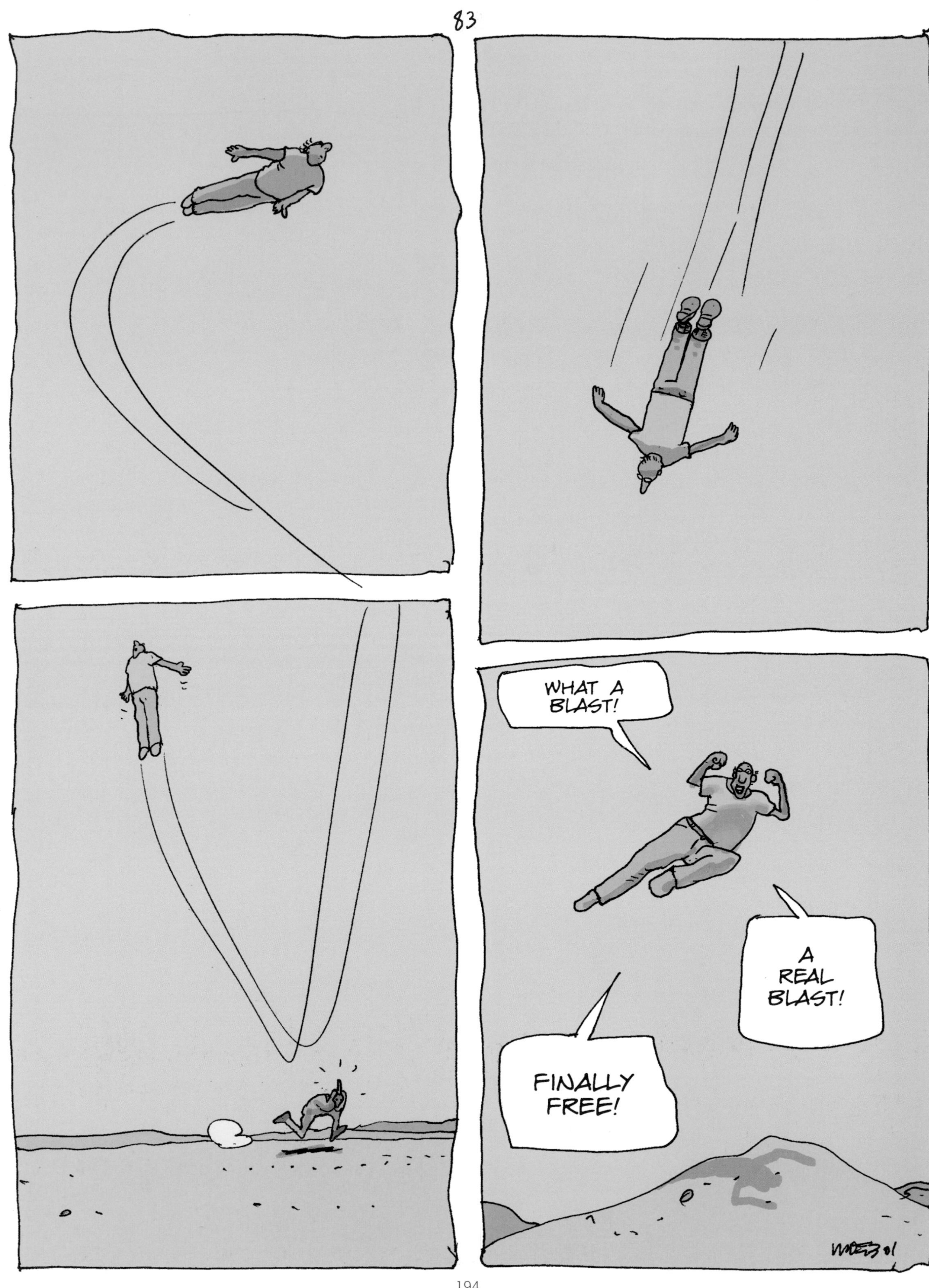
WHAT A BLAST!
A REAL BLAST!
FINALLY FREE!
MOEB 81

AND WHAT FUN IT IS TO FLY OVER DESERT "B," AS FREE AS A BIRD.

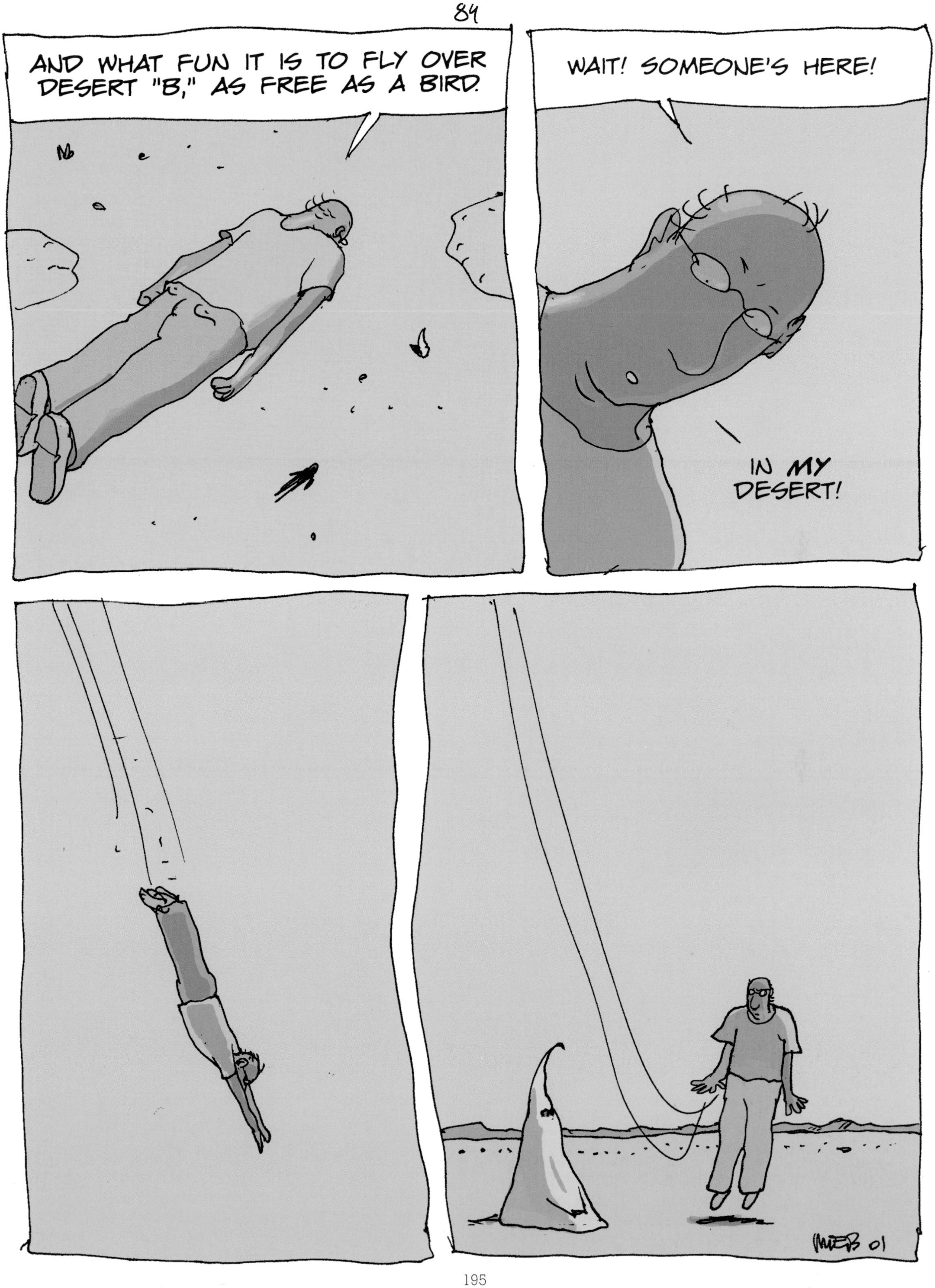

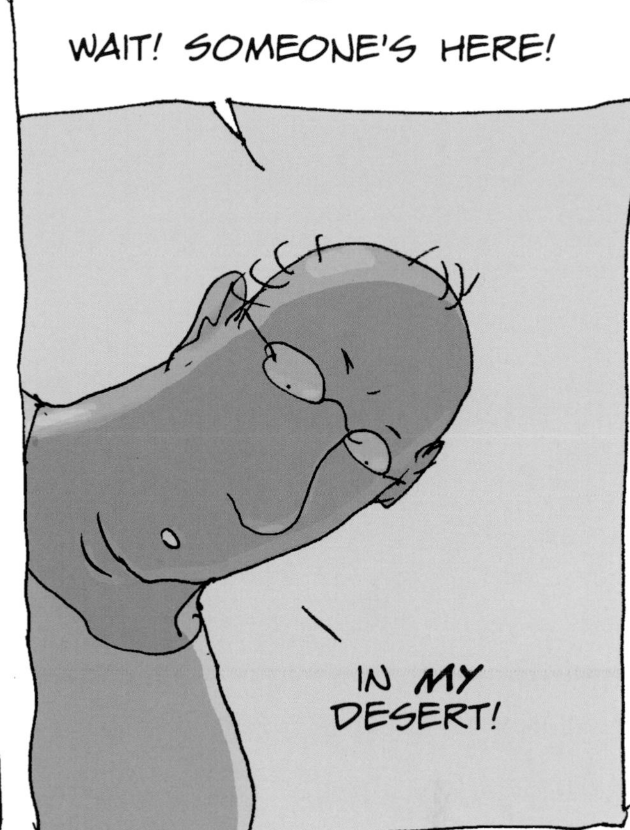
WAIT! SOMEONE'S HERE!
IN **MY** DESERT!

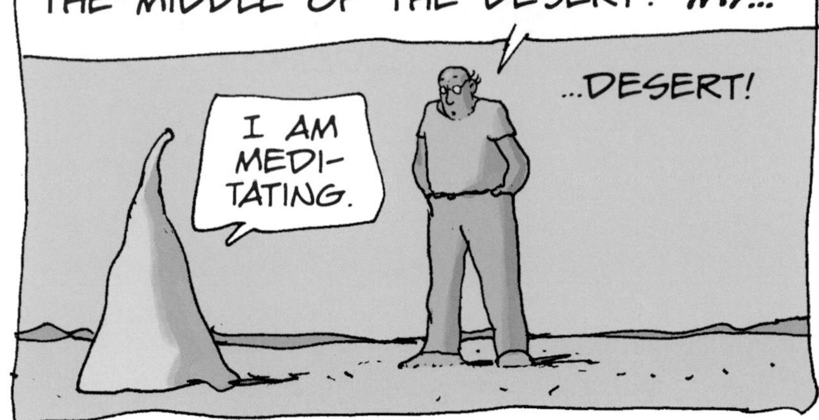

OH...MY FRIEND BIN?! WHAT ARE YOU DOING HERE, LIKE THIS, ALL ALONE IN THE MIDDLE OF THE DESERT? **MY...**
...DESERT!
I AM MEDI-TATING.

I HAVE BEEN PRAYING AND MEDITATING HERE FOR FORTY DAYS. I AM HUNGRY AND THIRSTY, AND MY ASS IS REALLY SORE.

ALL IN ALL, I AM FED UP, AND I WANT TO GO HOME.
NO PROB. WE'LL GET EVERYONE TOGETHER AT THE BUNKER... AND **PARTY!**

I'LL MAKE A BIG SALAD WITH RAW VEGGIES AND EXTRA VIRGIN OLIVE OIL WITH ORGANIC LEMON.
INSHALLAH!

BUT I WOULD RATHER RETURN TO AFGHAN-ISTAN...

YEAH, OF COURSE. I PROMISE, I'LL SEND YOU BACK HOME AFTER THE PARTY!

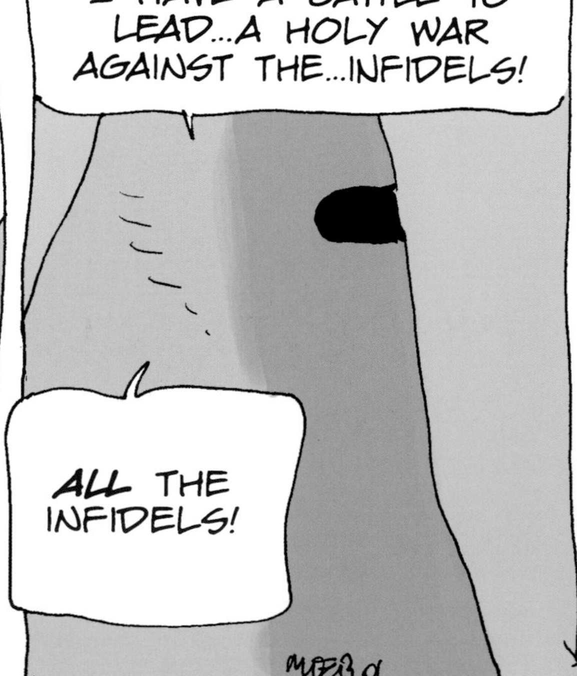

I HAVE A BATTLE TO LEAD...A HOLY WAR AGAINST THE...INFIDELS!
ALL THE INFIDELS!
MŒBIUS

THE WHOLE PLANET EARTH MUST BE THE PLANET OF ISLAM...ALL ITS PEOPLES IN PRAYER...ITS WOMEN VEILED AND MODEST, ITS CHILDREN READING OUR HOLY TEXTS. ***ISLAM*** WILL SAVE THE WORLD!

MY DEAR BIN, I DON'T BELIEVE YOU QUITE UNDERSTAND HOW THINGS WORK HERE, IN DESERT "B"... MY DESERT "B"...

...THE ILLUSION OF REALITY PREVAILS, BUT EVERYTHING YOU SAY AND DO IS UNDER THE AUTHOR'S ABSOLUTE CONTROL.

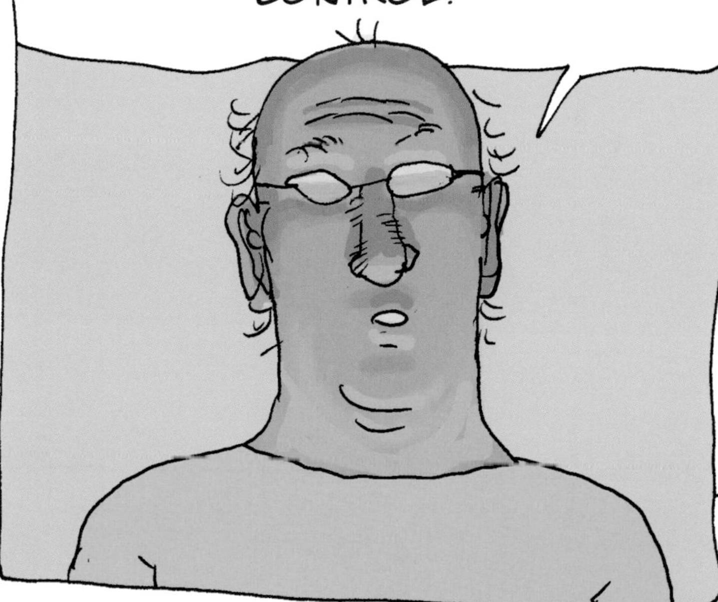

AND I KNOW WHAT I'M TALKING ABOUT--BECAUSE WHILE I'M SUPPOSED TO BE THE AUTHOR, EVEN ***I'M*** JUST A TWO-DIMENSIONAL DRAWING WITH NO WILL OF MY OWN...

IT IS WELL KNOWN THAT IMAGES ARE THE WORK OF SATAN!

TO TRUST AN IMAGE IS LIKE TRUSTING A MIRAGE.

YOU'RE MISTAKING ***IMAGE*** FOR ***IMAGINARY...*** AND YOU CAN'T GO HOME AGAIN, AS YOU'D LIKE. YOUR SELF IS LIVING ITS LIFE, BUT WITHOUT ***YOU***...THERE, IN THE AUTHOR AND READERS' WORLD.

IN THAT CASE YOU ARE WORTH NO MORE THAN I! YOU ARE NOTHING!
DON'T YOU BELIEVE IT! MOEB CREATED ME IN HIS OWN IMAGE! HE MORTIFIES ME, MISTREATS ME, AND MISREPRESENTS ME...

...BUT...HE **LOVES** ME!

HE DOESN'T LOVE **ME?**
OF COURSE NOT! YOU DON'T WANT TO BE LOVED.

IT IS TRUE. I WISH TO BE FEARED.
I THINK HE **IS** AFRAID OF YOU...YOU OR YOUR BUDDIES... FOR SURE!

IF HE FEARS ME, THEN I WISH HIM TO GIVE ME BACK MY MASCULINE FORM... OR I SHALL SET MY CUTTHROATS LOOSE ON HIM. THEY ARE EVERYWHERE! HE CANNOT HIDE!
I UNDER-STAND... HMM...

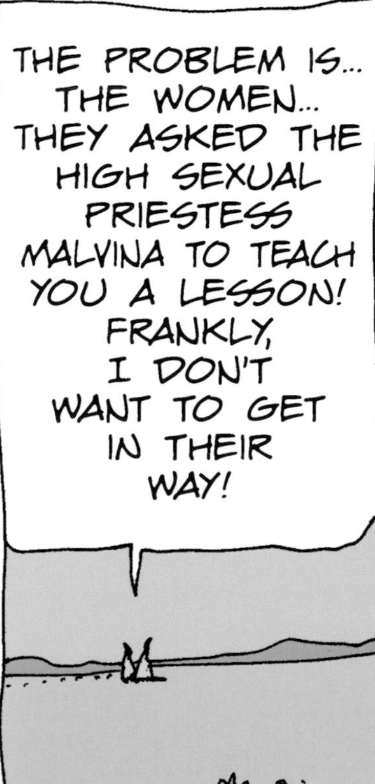
THE PROBLEM IS... THE WOMEN... THEY ASKED THE HIGH SEXUAL PRIESTESS MALVINA TO TEACH YOU A LESSON! FRANKLY, I DON'T WANT TO GET IN THEIR WAY!

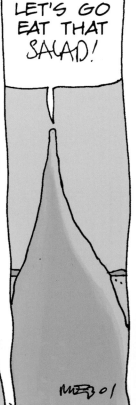

SORRY.
OK!
LET'S GO EAT THAT SALAD!

YOU SAY HE LOVES YOU, YES?

WELL, YEAH.

ALLOW ME TO ASK YOU A QUESTION, THEN...?

UH...GO AHEAD!

ARE YOU SURE HE LOVES **HIMSELF**?

...AT LEAST?!

OKAY...

WELL...

M.01

OBVIOUSLY HE LOVES HIMSELF! IF NOT, WHY WOULD HE GIVE ME ALL THESE PAGES...ALL OF DESERT "B"...?

HE'S ALSO LETTING ME FULFILL MY DREAM! UH... HIS DREAM!

IN ANY CASE, IT'S EVERYONE'S DREAM. DON'T MOVE! I'LL SHOW YOU.

DON'T MOVE. JUST WATCH...

M.01

M.01

IT'S LIKE BEING SUPERMAN!
I NEVER WANT IT TO END!
I'VE NEVER FLOWN SO EASILY, SO FAST, SO HIGH, SO FAR!
I KNOW WHAT TO DO... I'LL TRY TO GO TO THE EDGE OF THIS DREAM... TO THE LIMIT...
...OF DESERT "B."
HERE WE GO!
IT'LL TAKE THE TIME IT TAKES.
I HAVE A FEELING IT'S THE ONLY WAY TO KNOW IF HE TRULY LOVES ME...AND LOVES HIMSELF...
WHAT GOOD IS THIS COMIC IF IT'S NOT DICTATED BY LOVE?
M. 01

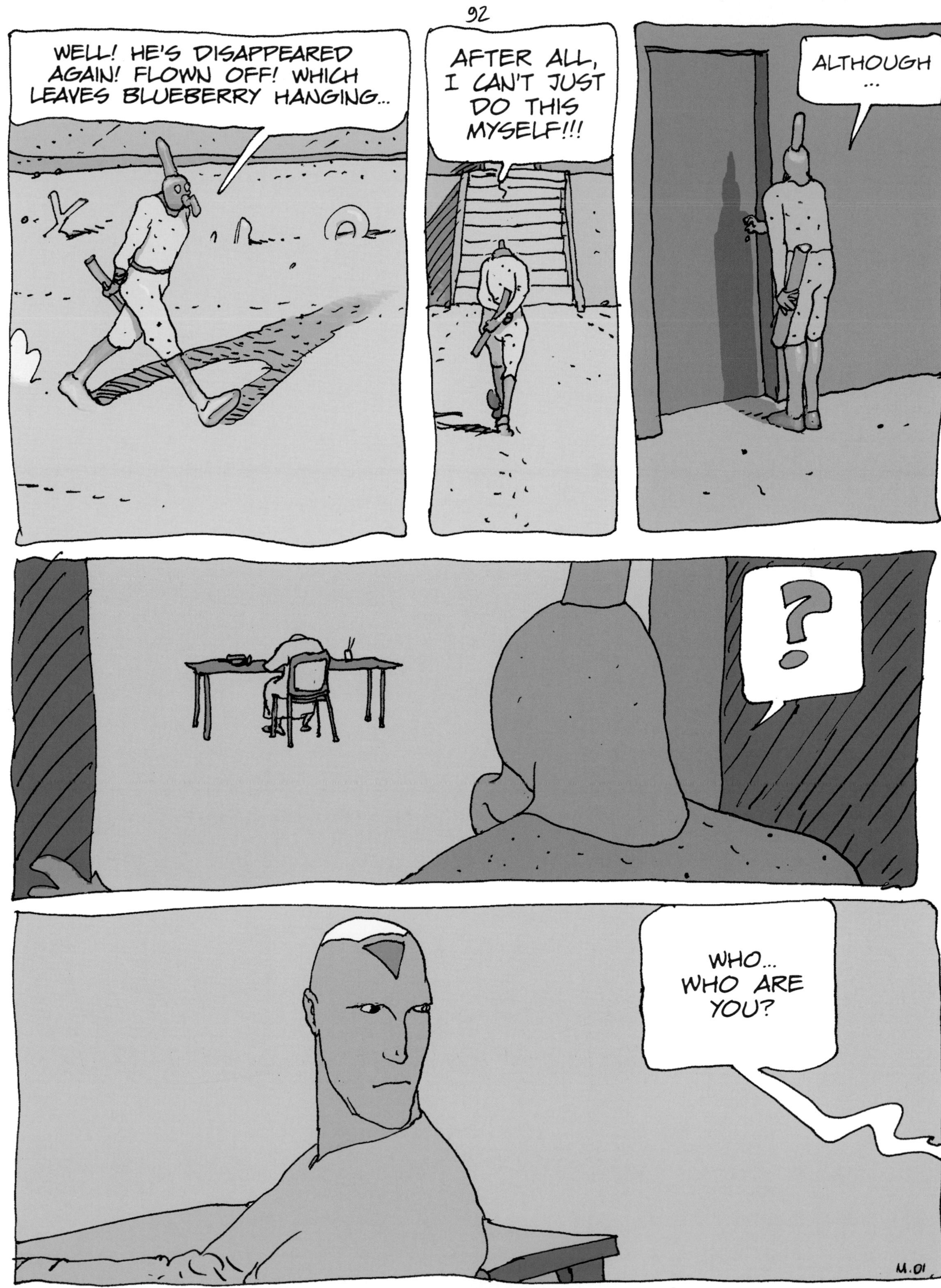
WELL! HE'S DISAPPEARED AGAIN! FLOWN OFF! WHICH LEAVES BLUEBERRY HANGING...
AFTER ALL, I CAN'T JUST DO THIS MYSELF!!!
ALTHOUGH ...
?
WHO... WHO ARE YOU?
M.01

WHAT A STORM!

I CAN'T SEE A THING! I DEFINITELY MUST BE GETTING NEAR THE EDGE.

I AM MASTER BURG.
OH, RIGHT! THE GARDENS... THE THING... EDENA!
M.01

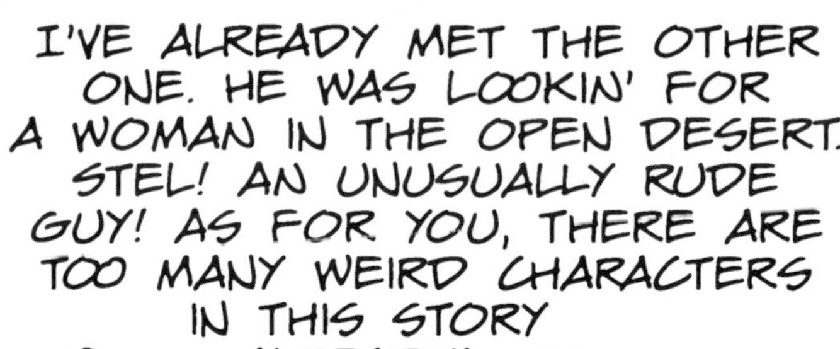
I'VE ALREADY MET THE OTHER ONE. HE WAS LOOKIN' FOR A WOMAN IN THE OPEN DESERT. STEL! AN UNUSUALLY RUDE GUY! AS FOR YOU, THERE ARE TOO MANY WEIRD CHARACTERS IN THIS STORY ALREADY!

WEIRD? ME? **YOU'RE** THE WEIRD ONE, WITH THAT BROKEN NOSE! AND THAT OUTFIT! WHERE'D YOU GET IT?

OH...UH...IT'S A COSTUME I FOUND ON THE FLOOR IN A HALLWAY...I'M ACTUALLY HERE INCOGNITO...
I SEE!

AAAND...WHERE'S THE AUTHOR? I DON'T SEE HIM ANYWHERE.
THE AUTHOR?

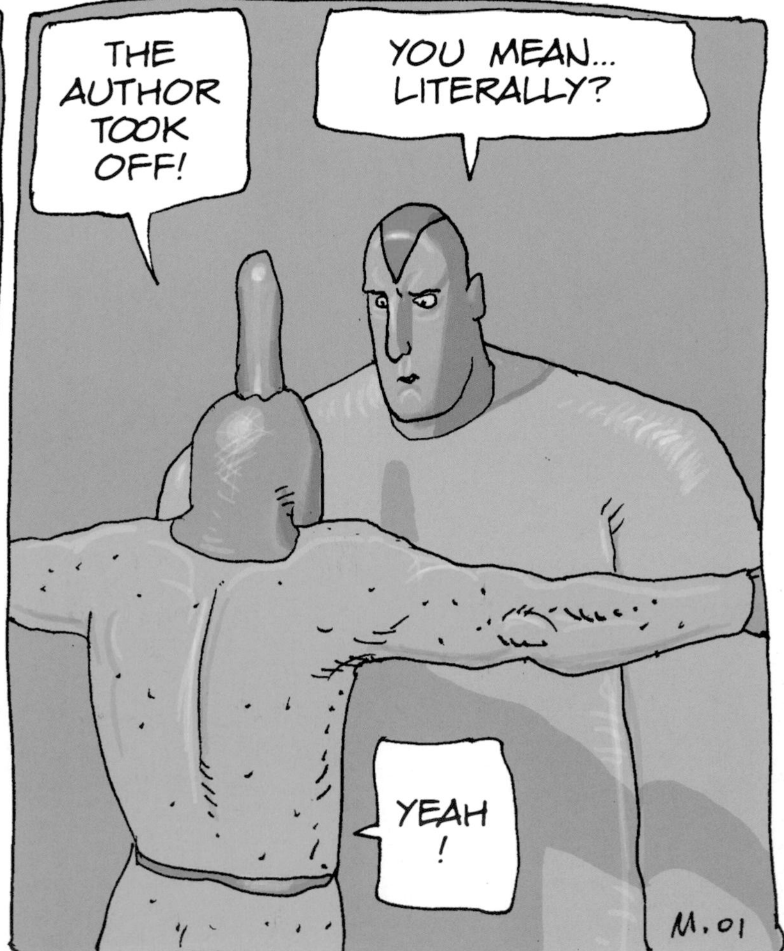
THE AUTHOR TOOK OFF!
YOU MEAN... LITERALLY?
YEAH!
M.01

THAT'S TROUBLESOME. THE DESIRE TO FLY IS TYPICAL IN MANIC-DEPRESSIVES!
BLOODY HELL! IT'S TRUE! HE'S EVEN DECIDED THAT HE'S GOD!

I KNEW IT'D BE BETTER TO STICK TO A GOOD OLD WESTERN, WHERE NO ONE EVER GETS IT INTO HIS HEAD TO FLY... NOT TO MENTION **THE SALES!**
LET'S NOT EXAGGERATE!

WHAT DO YOU MEAN? AM I EXAGGERATIN'?
WELL, FOR EXAMPLE, DID YOU KNOW THAT THE ***XIII*** SERIES SOLD ALMOST A MILLION COPIES?

I KNOW...AND IT MAKES ME SICK! BUT WHAT CAN YOU DO? HE DOESN'T WORK ENOUGH! HIS SCRIPTS ARE HOPELESS, AND HIS STYLE'S GETTIN' OLD!
YOU'RE THE ONE EXAGGERATING ***NOW,*** MY FRIEND! IT MIGHT ALSO JUST BE THE LIMITATION OF THE WESTERN GENRE. DON'T ***PANIC!*** THE REAL QUESTION IS: ***WHERE IS MOEB?***

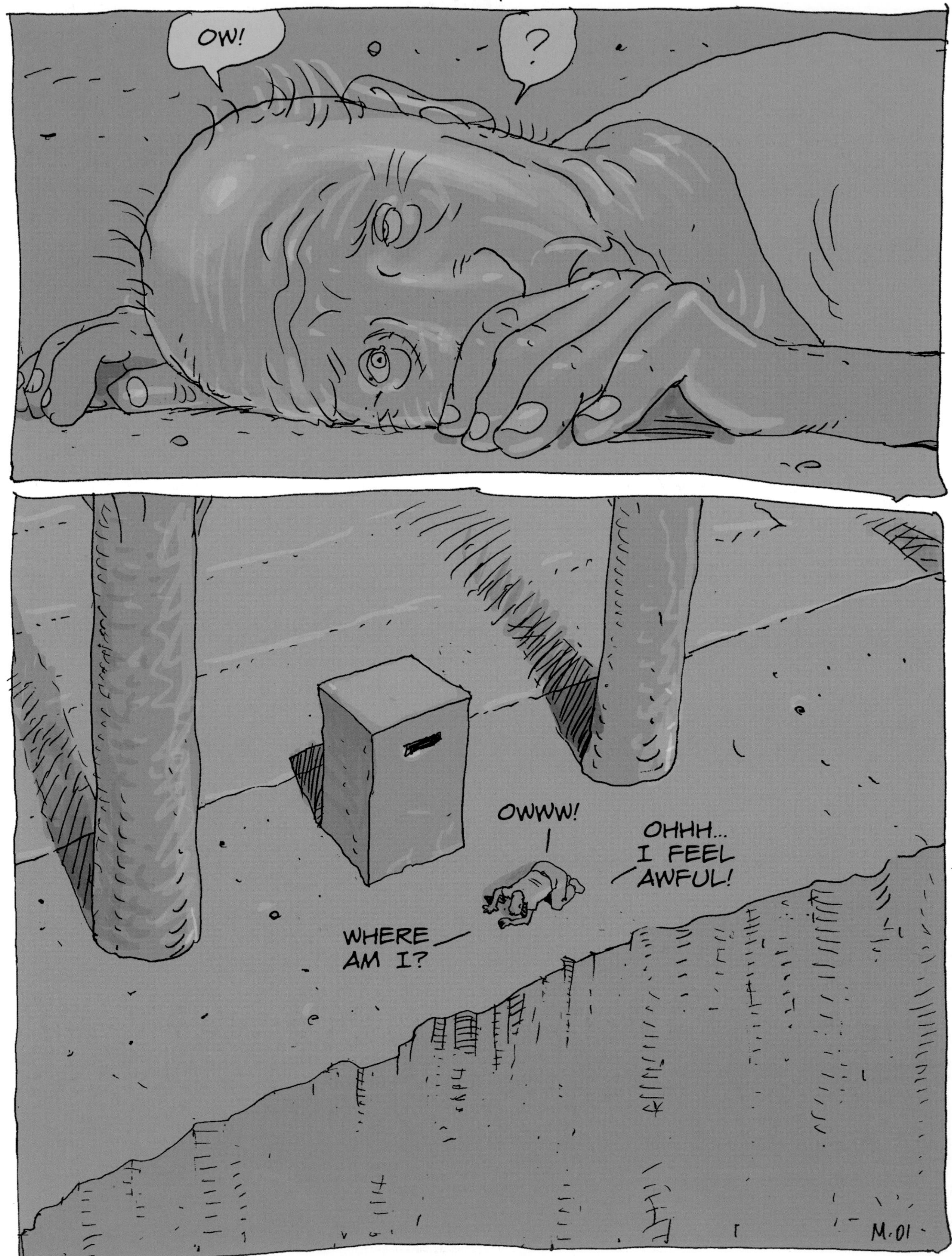
OW!
?
OWWW!
OHHH...
I FEEL
AWFUL!
WHERE
AM I?
M.01

MY GLASSES! SHIT! I MUST HAVE BLACKED OUT!

WHAT IS THIS STRANGE PLACE?
AND THAT SPACE... THAT HOLE... WHAT IS IT?

?!

OH... NOoo!

GOOD GOD! BLACK! SOLID BLACK IN MY COMIC BOOK! AND WHAT WAS IT? THE RIVER STYX? THE PROEFOUND OEMPTINESS OF SPÆCE?
IN ANY CASE...IT'S A BAD SIGN.
M.01

A ROAD! TREES?! NO QUESTION--IT'S THE EXTREME EDGE! I'VE COME TO THE END OF "B."

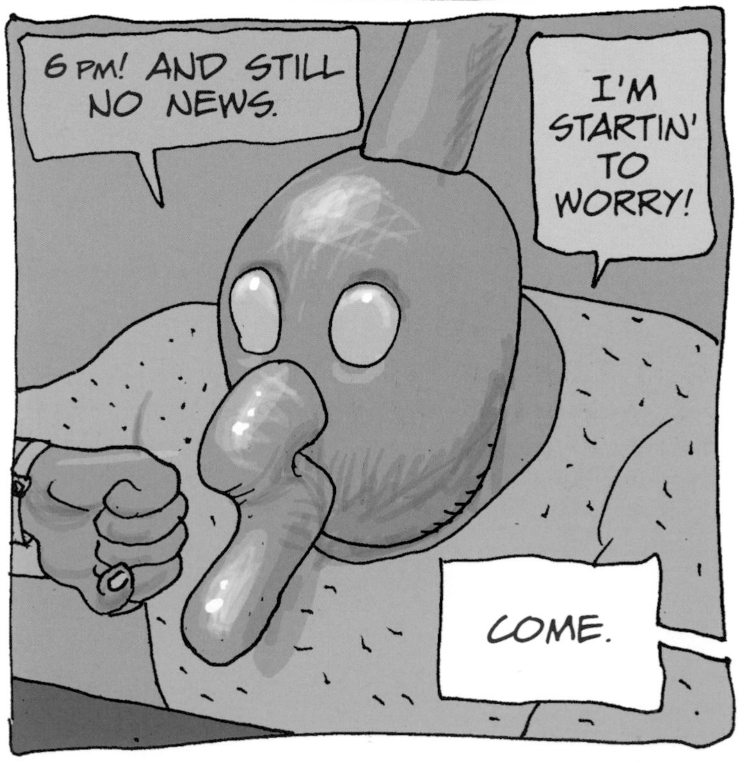

6 PM! AND STILL NO NEWS.
I'M STARTIN' TO WORRY!
COME.

WE'LL MAKE A SALAD! A BIG SALAD WITH A SPRINKLING OF EXTRA VIRGIN OLIVE OIL...
A COLD SALAD!
RIGHT! WITH FRUIT! LOTS OF FRUIT!
M.01

BUS

B LINE

I FEEL WORSE AND WORSE.

IT WAS THE BLACK! ALL THAT **BLACK!**

I WANT TO THROW UP!

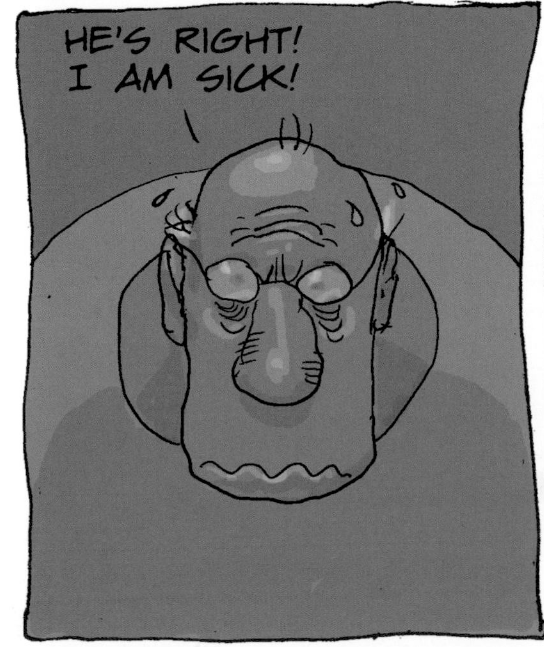

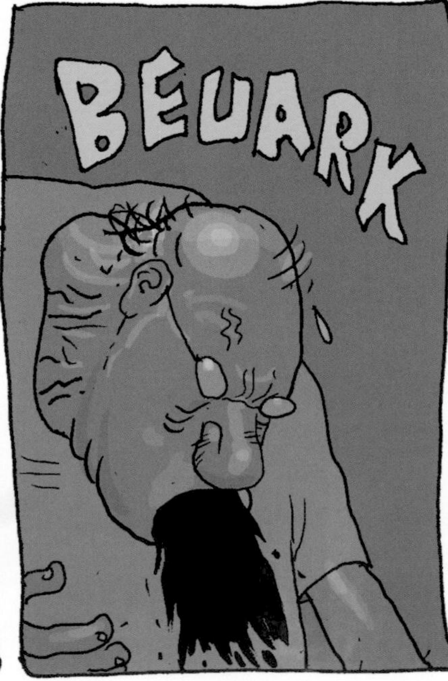

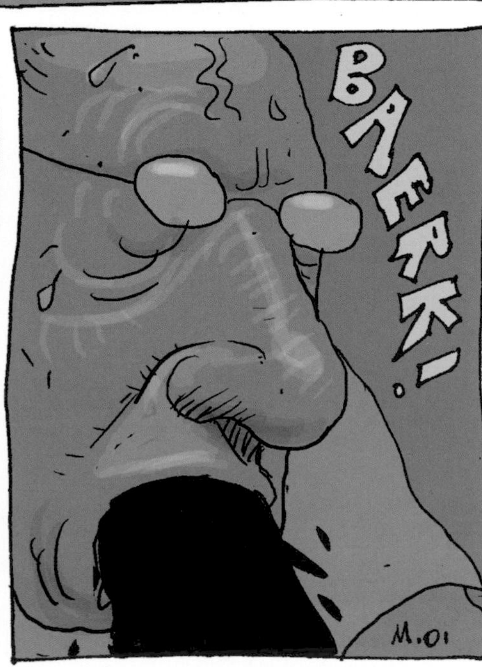

SIR! YOU THREW UP BLACK!
I THREW UP! IN FACT, I THREW UP BLACK.
DAD! HE THREW UP BLACK!

WHAT...ARE YOU GONNA DO WITH THOSE SNAKES?
YOUR HEART MUST BE PURIFIED.
WE MUST KNOW THE SOURCE OF THE BLACK!

NO!
WE MUST.

BREATHE CALMLY.
ARGH!
EARKGG!
M. 01

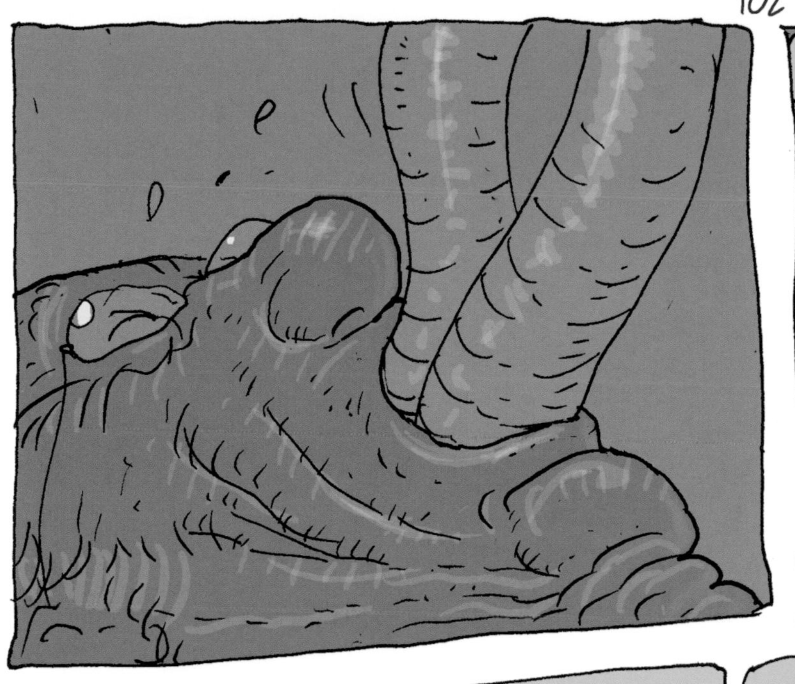

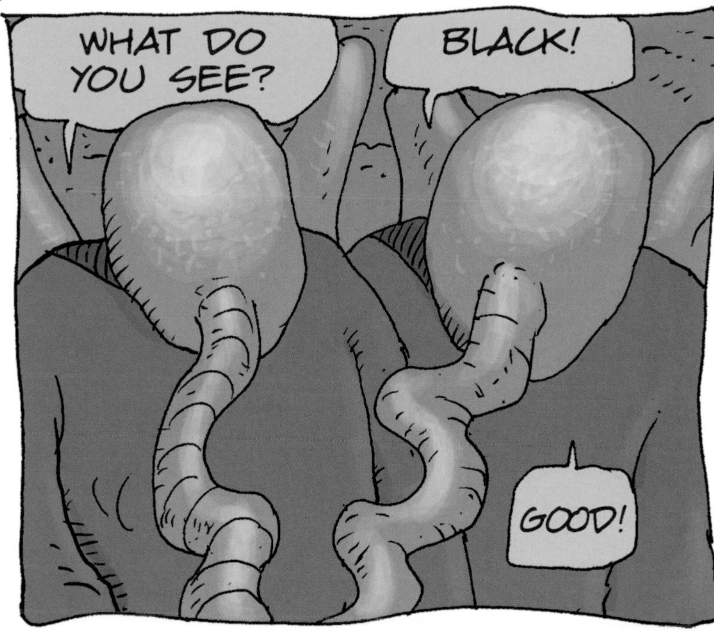

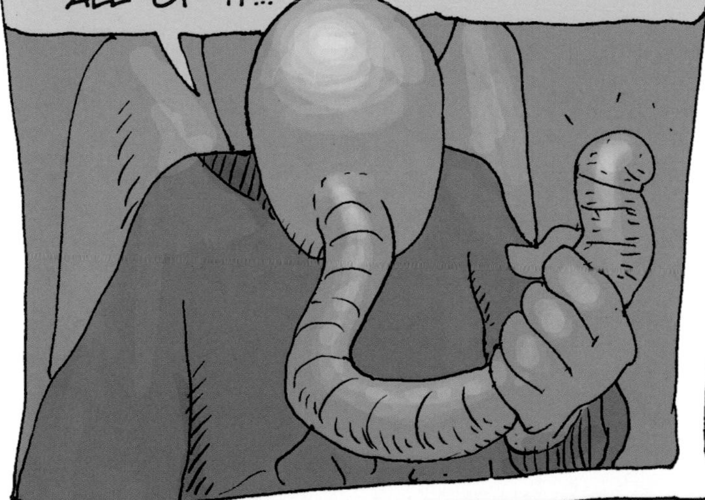

*THE REAL DEAL.

GOOD GRIEF! EVERYTHING WAS GOING SO WELL! FLYING LIKE AN EAGLE AND THEN SUDDENLY-- LIGHTNING! THE FALL! THE BLACK!

I SHOULD NEVER HAVE TRIED TO TOUCH THE LIMITS OF THE DREAM! THAT'S WHAT MADE ME FALL! ON THE OTHER HAND, THAT'S ALSO WHAT MADE ME FLY!

HOW IS IT THAT THINGS CAN BE BOTH GOOD AND BAD AT THE SAME TIME?

HEY, YOU! THE AUTHOR!

I'LL DRIVE YOU!

C'MON.

BUT...WHO ARE YOU?

M. 01

BUT...YOU'RE DITCHING THE ROAD?!

ALWAYS !!!

YOU'RE SURE IT'S THIS WAY?

DON'T ASK IDIOTIC QUESTIONS...TRY TO RELAX INSTEAD!

RELAX?

WITH ALL THAT WORK WAITING FOR ME? BLUEBERRY, ARZAK, ETC., ETC....

M.01

NO WAY I'M GIVING UP!
HHNNGH!
HNNH!
STOP FOOLING AROUND!
I TOLD YOU...YOU'RE IN NO SHAPE TO FLY! SIT DOWN AND TRY TO RELAX.
SLEEP!
SLEEP!
NEVER.
M.01

I'D RATHER DIE.
NO! WAIT!

WHAT *IS* SHE THINKING, THAT WOMAN?
NOTHING CAN KEEP ME FROM FLYING IN DESERT "B."

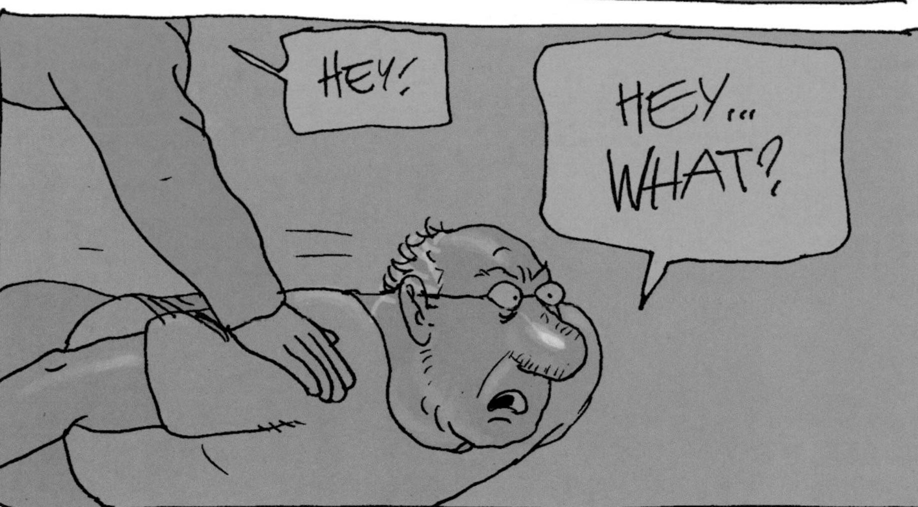
HEY!
HEY... WHAT?

WAKE UP! WE'RE HERE!
BUT...
M. 01

SO!

GO ON IN! WHAT ARE YOU WAITING FOR?

I... I DON'T KNOW! I'M WAVERING...

M. 01

THE QUESTION IS: DOES HE LOVE ME?
8
END OF PART 1
TO BE CONTINUED...
M.01

INSIDE MOEBIUS PART 1 TRANSLATOR'S NOTES

Literary translation is a tricky business. It's one thing to know what the original words mean; it's quite another to know what the *author* meant by those words. And in the case of Moebius, this can be a complex proposition indeed! The translator's job typically involves putting oneself inside the head of the author, and Moebius took his own head into some very unusual places, stretching his consciousness in fascinating and provocative ways. *Inside Moebius* is appropriately named, as the legendary artist brings the reader directly into this exploration of his own creative thought processes.

People who speak only one language seldom realize just how much *writing* is involved in literary translation. The words on the translated page must not only convey the various shades of meaning, but voice, tone, and characterization as well. And in comics, those words also have to fit the prescribed space of the caption or balloon. I often annotate my translation scripts, explaining certain word choices and/or providing alternatives. Editor Philip R. Simon thought those notes might interest the reader, so we've included some of them here.

—Diana Schutz, 2017

Page 6—FOREWORD
The name of Moebius's inner creative landscape, Desert B, has its source in the artist's typically ingenious wordplay: to stop smoking weed is, indeed, to *weed oneself out.* The French term for *to weed* (as in *weeding a garden*) is *désherber*, and the pronunciation of *désherber* is identical, in French, to that of *Désert B.* Additionally, when inverted, the two initial capitals of *Désert B* become *BD*, short for *bande dessinée*, the French term for *comics.*

Page 9—"Possible Vanishing Point"
The French title of this section of the foreword is another bit of wordplay, because it can mean three different things: Possible Point of Escape; No Escape Possible; and Possible Vanishing Point. The latter itself can refer, in graphical perspective, to that point in the image plane where receding parallel lines appear to converge, a point beyond which they essentially vanish. But the term can also refer, more generally, to that point at which *anything* disappears or ceases to exist. Despite the appeal of the idea of escape, or—maybe better—its impossibility, *Inside Moebius* is indeed "a study of point of view and of the effects of perspective," and the author's struggles with his own mortality form a clear theme of the book. Consequently, "Possible Vanishing Point" became my choice here.

Page 33
The original French describes Moebius here as *dégrisé*, a term meaning both *sober* and *brought down to earth*: more of the author's clever wordplay.

Pages 35 & 36
Unfortunately, the lettering in these thumbnails is so small that the words are illegible in places.

Page 37
Bon sang is a very mild expletive in French whose literal meaning is *good blood.* As with many French expletives, it derives from Roman Catholicism—in this case, the blood of Christ. Equivalent English expressions might include *hell's bells*, *damn* or *damn it*, *bother* or *bugger*, or any similar interjection beginning with *good*: *good heavens*, *good Lord*, and so on. In deference to Charles Schulz's *Peanuts*, I decided to go with *good grief* any time *bon sang* appears in the original script.

Page 47
A reformed alcoholic, Matt Scudder is a detective character in a series of novels by Lawrence Block.

Page 60

Puns are, of course, impossible to translate, and Moebius loves them! The best a translator can do is try to get close or give a similar flavor. In this case, Major Grubert chides Blueberry for *making a fuss over a simple story*. Moebius uses the French idiom *faire des histoires* for *making a fuss*, so the original line translates, literally, as *making stories over a simple story*. The story in question is the then-unfinished script for *OK Corral*, which would eventually become volume 27 of the *Blueberry* series.

Page 69

The first line on this page is undoubtedly an allusion to both the famous 1921 play by Italian playwright Luigi Pirandello, *Six Characters in Search of an Author*, and to Milo Manara's riff on Pirandello, "An Author in Search of Six Characters" (published in volume 5 of *The Manara Library* from Dark Horse Comics). Moebius was certainly aware of both the Pirandello play *and* the Manara story.

Page 73

The conversion from kilograms to pounds is not exact. The original French text refers to 50-kilo bags of marbles, which would actually be about 110 lbs. I've elected to follow Moebius's preference here for nicely rounded-off numbers; hence, 100 lbs.

Jeannot is the French diminutive for *Jean* [Giraud], just as, for example, *Johnny* is the English diminutive for *John*.

Fontenay-sous-Bois is the northern suburb of Paris where Moebius was raised by his grandparents. *Rue Pasteur* simply means *Pasteur Street*.

Page 75

The Jean-Michel discussed on this page is Jean-Michel Charlier, Belgian writer and co-creator of the *Blueberry* series of graphic novels. If Wikipedia is correct, he actually died in 1989, not 1990, as the older Moebius claims on this page.

Page 76

Jacques Chirac was the President of France from May 1995 to May 2007. These pages of *Inside Moebius Part 1*, originally published in French, are dated 2001, which means Moebius would have been working on them at about the halfway point of Chirac's term in office.

François Mitterrand preceded Chirac as French President, from May 1981 to May 1995.

In the original French, Moebius refers to a *zing* crashing into the Pentagon and the *bings* that caused throughout the world. The term *zinc* is WWII slang for a plane, and *bings* is onomatopoeia for the kind of noise resulting, for instance, from a huge shock. Moebius is playing on the rhyme here, using *zing* for *zinc*. I followed him by using the slang *bird* for *plane* but opted then to extend the metaphor rather than force a rhyme. Thanks to Edward Gauvin for cluing me into the slang meaning of *zinc*.

Page 98

According to Wikipedia-France, Patrick Cauvin was the pseudonym of the late Claude Klotz, a French writer and novelist. Gir, of course, was another pen name used by Jean Giraud.

Page 112

This single page is the triple whammy of all wordplay, and no English word comes even remotely close to carrying the many connotations of the original, so I've elected to leave it as is. Although we generally use the term in English to refer to photo comics, *fumetti* is actually the Italian word for *comics*, any kind of comics. It's derived from the word *fumo*, which means *smoke*. *Fumetti* literally means *little smokes*, or *little puffs of smoke*, which is how the Italians got their word for comics in the first place, since the "clouds" used to indicate speech in comics—word balloons, that is—can be said to resemble little puffs of smoke or *fumetti*. In fact, Mort Walker's *Lexicon of Comicana*, the *Beetle Bailey* cartoonist's charming, but specialized, glossary of comics iconography, also uses the collective term *fumetti* for all the various types of word

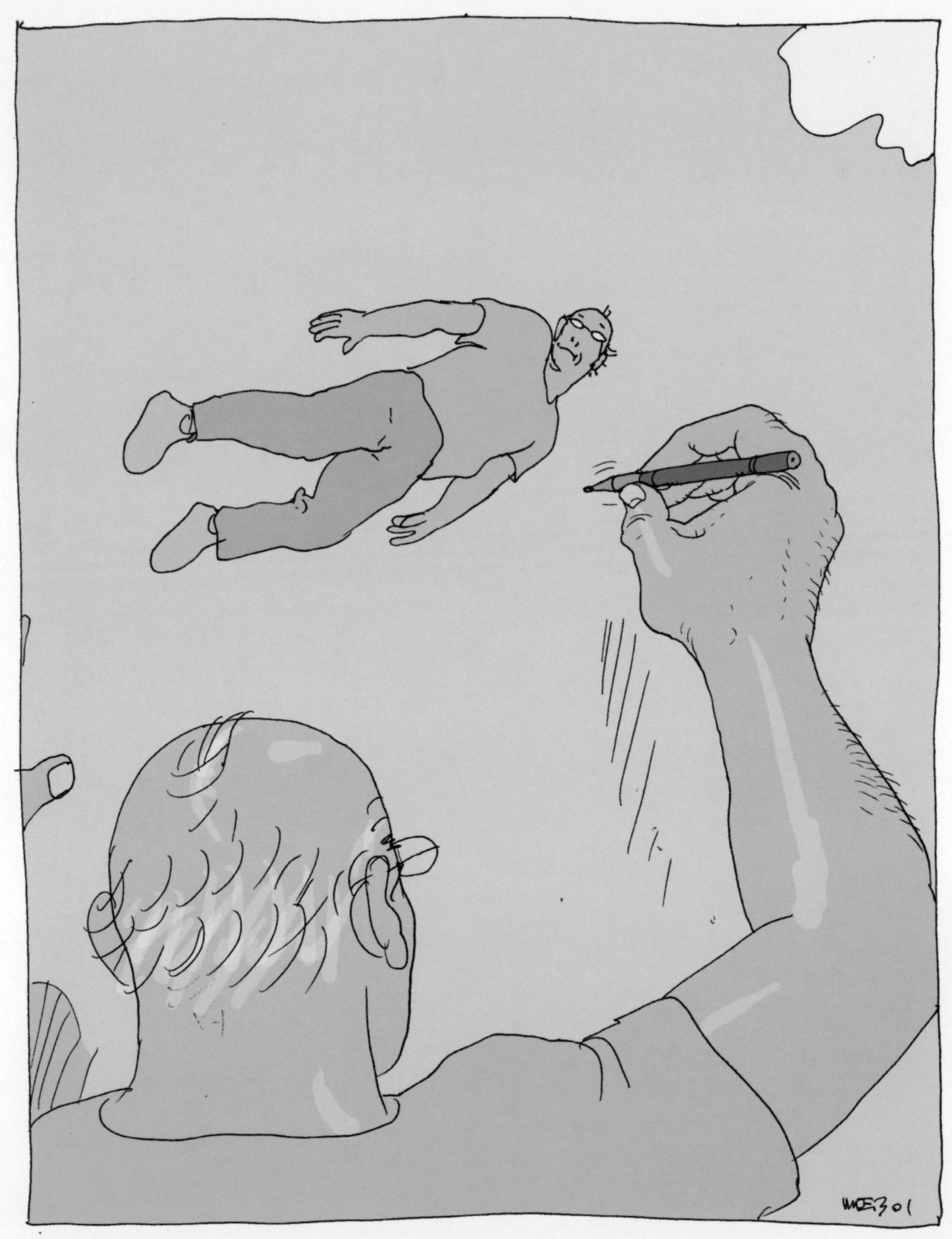

balloons. *Fumée*, the French noun for *smoke*, is similar enough to the Italian that the Moebius character on this page is clearly referencing the two small clouds of smoke he sees in the distance—the burning of the Twin Towers—while at the same time using a word that French readers recognize as a term for *comics*. But it gets better. The French slang term *fumette*, a word almost identical to *fumetti*, refers to *pot* or to *smoking pot*, the author's abstention from which provides the very springboard for this graphic novel. Triple whammy, like I said.

Page 125

More information on the Tar'hai and the Bakalite can be found in *The Airtight Garage*. Major Grubert is allied with the "twenty-three generating divinities that are the sacred pillars of the Tar'hai Mythology."

Page 147

The English word *assassin* is derived from *Hashishin*, a secretive murder cult originating in the eleventh century. Sources disagree as to whether the cult actually used hashish or not.

Page 163

La mine de l'allemand perdu (routinely, though incorrectly, translated as *The Lost Dutchman's Mine* to accord with the name of an actual American legend) and *Chihuaha Pearl* are, respectively, the eleventh and thirteenth *Blueberry* volumes in the series.

Page 174

The term *bis* is Latin for *two* or *twice*. This, in fact, is the derivation of our prefix "bi–": as in *bifurcate* or *bilateral*. In the story, Moebius says that *Bis* is "the second world" or "the second Earth" . . . which, of course, makes the "Earth-Two" translation absolutely irresistible to a comics nerd like me.

Uses of the ligature—here, in *Gœd*, and elsewhere in the story—are, of course, a play on the ligature in *Moebius*.

Page 176

Christian Bobin is a French author and poet. The original French quote is: *Les seuls suicides réussis sont les suicides ratés.*

Page 177

This authentic "Sacred Land" presumably refers to Mecca and Medina, in Saudi Arabia.

Page 178

Jean Giraud's youngest daughter is indeed named after the eponymous character of *Nausicaä of the Valley of the Wind*, by Japanese cartoonist and animator Hayao Miyazaki.

Page 185

Inshallah is Arabic for *God willing*. In other words: *If Allah wills.*

Page 207

Jean Giraud drew the first volume of the two-part *XIII: La Version Irlandaise* (*XIII: The Irish Version*), from a script by Jean Van Hamme.

Page 215

The last panel on this page is, I believe, a direct reference to Moebius's 1973 story "La Déviation," which was originally translated as "The Detour."

BIOGRAPHY

Jean Giraud was born in 1938 in Nogent-sur-Marne, France. He started his career at age sixteen, working for a children's magazine, and then he began illustrating for other French comics magazines—such as *Far West*, *Bonux-Boy*, and *Coeurs vaillants*—around 1957. After a remarkable trip to Mexico, where he encountered the desert landscapes that would inspire him throughout his life, he collaborated with Joseph Gillain (a.k.a. Jijé) in 1961 on the *Jerry Spring* western series. This experiment would help him grow into the style he used in the *Pilote* journal in France, where he drew under the pen name Gir and co-created the successful, long-running *Blueberry* series with writer Jean-Michel Charlier. Giraud created the name for the title, and the complete *Blueberry* series ran for approximately thirty collected volumes.

Simultaneously, Giraud began publishing under another pen name—Moebius. In the strips drawn with this name, he embraced new inspirations and turned toward humor, fantasy, and science-fiction stories. After cofounding the Humanoïdes Associés publishing house, which launched *Heavy Metal* magazine (*Métal hurlant* in France) in 1975, Jean Giraud continued to develop a unique and innovative style under the name Moebius. In *Arzach* (1975) and *The Airtight Garage* (1976), he revolutionized the creative aspect of comics. With Alejandro Jodorowsky, he told the story of John Difool in *The Incal* (1980), a series that would place the team among the most innovative science-fiction storytellers of their time. Read worldwide, Moebius's work was noticed by great film directors, with whom he worked on several movies, including *Alien* by Ridley Scott, *Time Masters* by René Laloux, *Tron* by Steven Lisberger, *The Abyss* by James Cameron, and *The Fifth Element* by Luc Besson. In the US, Giraud started his own publishing house, Starwatcher, and he also completed several mainstream projects, such as *Silver Surfer: Parable* with Marvel Comics' Stan Lee (1988). In 1999, he helped to create the unique Airtight Garage game arcade in San Francisco.

In France in 1997, Jean Giraud started the Moebius Production/Stardom publishing house with his wife, Isabelle, consolidating all of his activities and publishing his work internationally in art books, silk-screen prints, portfolios, limited editions, products, and several collections, such as *40 jours dans le désert B* (1999), *Le chasseur déprime* (2008), and the *Inside Moebius* series (2004-2010), which is a profound and sardonic meditation on his relationship with the multidimensional universe he created and the characters found in it. During this time, he had major art exhibitions in Europe and Asia, but it was not until 2010 in Paris that he was the subject of a retrospective exhibition, held by the Fondation Cartier and titled *Moebius-Transe-Forme*. He died in his home in Montrouge, France, on March 10, 2012, at the age of seventy-three.

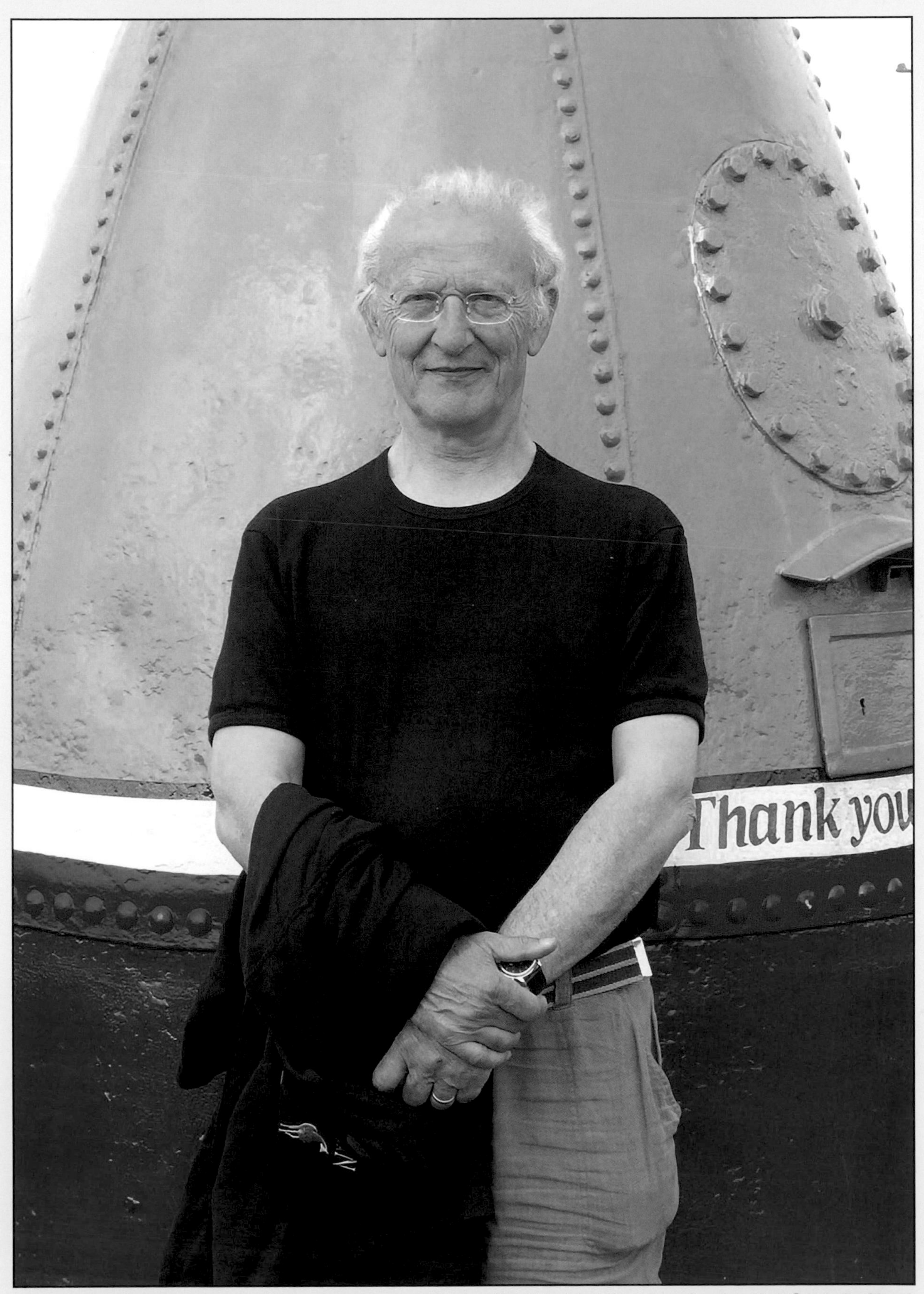

Jean "Moebius" Giraud, Los Angeles, 2010. © Isabelle Giraud.

SELECT BIBLIOGRAPHY OF MOEBIUS WORKS

WORKS TRANSLATED INTO ENGLISH

The Collected Fantasies of Jean Giraud

Moebius Volume 0: The Horny Goof & Other Underground Stories
(Dark Horse, 1990)

Moebius Volume 1/2: The Early Moebius & Other Humorous Stories
(Graphitti Designs, 1991)

Moebius Volume 1: Upon A Star
(Marvel/Epic, 1987)

Moebius Volume 2: Arzach & Other Fantasy Stories
(Marvel/Epic, 1987)

Moebius Volume 3: The Airtight Garage
(Marvel/Epic, 1987)

Moebius Volume 4: The Long Tomorrow & Other Science Fiction Stories
(Marvel/Epic, 1988)

Moebius Volume 5: The Gardens of Aedena
(Marvel/Epic, 1988)

Moebius Voume 6: Pharagonesia & Other Strange Stories
(Marvel/Epic, 1988)

Moebius Volume 7: The Goddess
(Marvel/Epic, 1990)

Moebius Volume 8: Mississippi River
(Marvel/Epic, 1990)

Moebius Volume 9: Stel
(Marvel/Epic, 1994)

Additional English-Language Graphic Novels

Moebius: Arzach
(Dark Horse, 1996)

Moebius: The Man from the Ciguri
(Dark Horse, 1996)

Moebius: Madwoman of the Sacred Heart
(Dark Horse, 1996, in collaboration with writer Alejandro Jodorowsky)

Moebius: H.P.'s Rock City
(Dark Horse, 1996)

Moebius: The Exotics
(Dark Horse, 1997)

Madwoman of the Sacred Heart (Humanoids, 2010, in collaboration with writer Alejandro Jodorowsky)

The Incal (Humanoids, 2011, in collaboration with writer Alejandro Jodorowsky)

The Eyes of the Cat
(Humanoids, 2012, in collaboration with writer Alejandro Jodorowsky)

Before the Incal (Humanoids, 2014, in collaboration with writer Alejandro Jodorowsky)

Moebius Library: The World of Edena
(Dark Horse, 2016)

Moebius Library: The Art of Edena
(Dark Horse, 2018)

Moebius Library: Inside Moebius Part 1
(Dark Horse, 2018)

WORKS IN FRENCH FROM STARDOM / MOEBIUS PRODUCTION

Tout Inside Moebius
Arzak, L'Arpenteur
Arzak, Tassili, tome 1
et sa version collector
Le chasseur déprime
Inside Moebius tomes 1 à ***6***
40 jours dans le désert B
2001 après Jésus Christ
Folles perspectives
X libris
Une jeunesse heureuse
Blueberry's
Portfolios:
Mourir et Voir Naples,
Mystère Montrouge, et
Les Jardins d'Eros 1

MOEBIUS LIBRARY:

The World of Edena

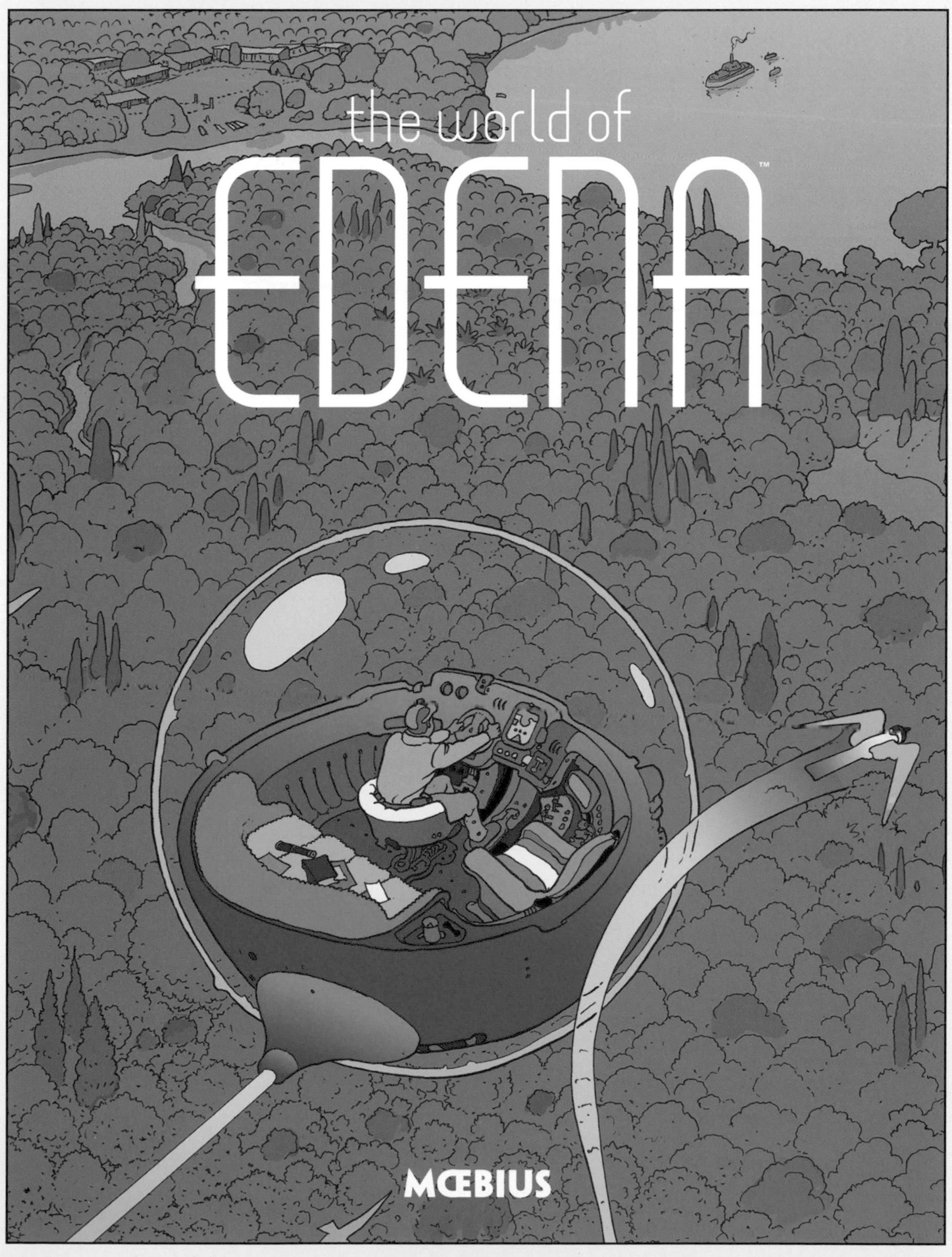

Available Now

MOEBIUS LIBRARY:

The Art of Edena

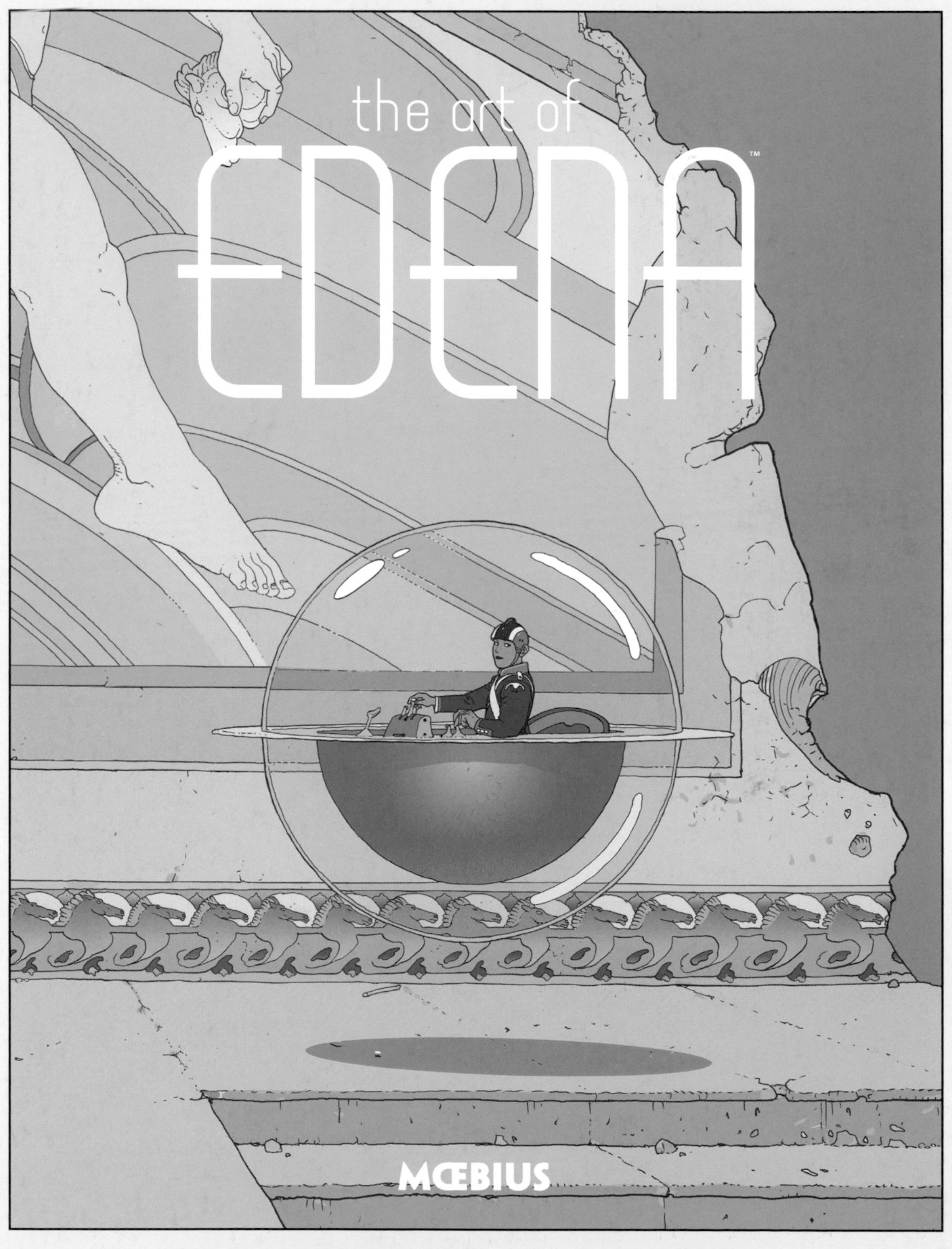

Available in 2018

MOEBIUS LIBRARY:

Inside Moebius Parts 1 to 3

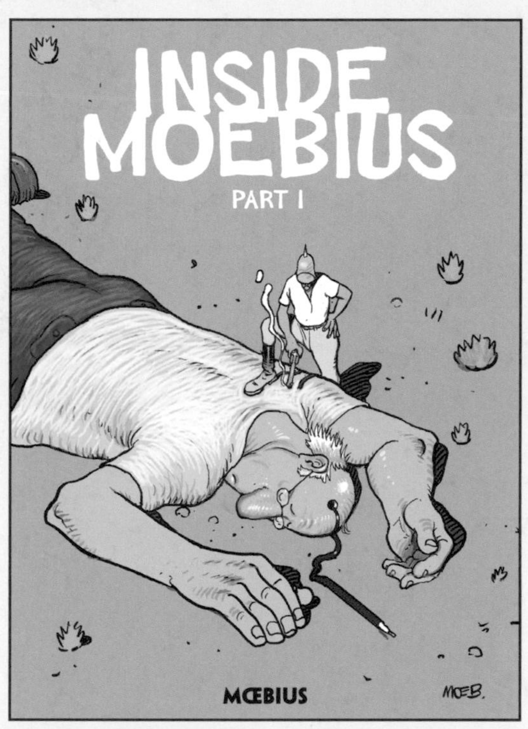

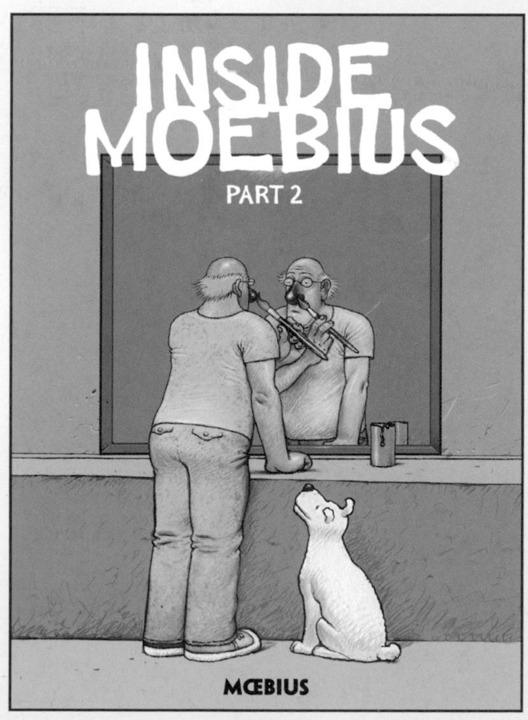

Three Volumes in 2018

Y YAAAAAOoooo...

AVON FREE PUBLIC LIBRARY
3 2529 14498 4226 
AVON FREE PUBLIC LIBRARY
281 COUNTRY CLUB ROAD, AVON CT 06001